HGTV KITCHENS

EDITOR: Amy Tincher-Durik
SENIOR ASSOCIATE DESIGN DIRECTOR: Doug Samuelson
PROJECT EDITORS AND WRITERS: Amber Dawn Barz, Jan Soults Walker
CONTRIBUTING ART DIRECTORS: Chris Conyers, Beth Runcie, Joe Wysong (Conyers Design, Inc.)
COPY CHIEF: Terri Fredrickson
PUBLISHING OPERATIONS MANAGER: Karen Schirm
EDIT AND DESIGN PRODUCTION COORDINATOR: Mary Lee Gavin
EDITORIAL ASSISTANTS: Kaye Chabot, Kairee Mullen
MARKETING PRODUCT MANAGERS: Aparna Pande, Isaac Petersen, Gina Rickert, Stephen Rogers, Brent Wiersma, Tyler Woods
BOOK PRODUCTION MANAGERS: Pam Kvitne, Marjorie J. Schenkelberg, Rick von Holdt, Mark Weaver
CONTRIBUTING STYLISTS: Cathy Kramer (Cathy Kramer Designs), Robin Tucker
PHOTOGRAPHERS: Edmund Barr, John Ellis, Michael Garland, Ken Gutmaker, Andy Lyons, Cameron Sadeghpour
CONTRIBUTING COPY EDITOR: Stacey Schildroth
CONTRIBUTING PROOFREADERS: Becky Etchen, Willa Speiser, Anne Terpstra
ILLUSTRATOR: Chad Johnston, Tom Stocki (The Art Factory)
INDEXER: Kathleen Poole

MEREDITH® BOOKS

EXECUTIVE DIRECTOR, EDITORIAL: Gregory H. Kayko
EXECUTIVE DIRECTOR, DESIGN: Matt Strelecki
EXECUTIVE EDITOR/GROUP MANAGER: Denise L. Caringer
PUBLISHER AND EDITOR IN CHIEF: James D. Blume
EDITORIAL DIRECTOR: Linda Raglan Cunningham
EXECUTIVE DIRECTOR, MARKETING: Jeffrey B. Myers
EXECUTIVE DIRECTOR, NEW BUSINESS DEVELOPMENT: Todd M. Davis
EXECUTIVE DIRECTOR, SALES: Ken Zagor
DIRECTOR, OPERATIONS: George A. Susral
DIRECTOR, PRODUCTION: Douglas M. Johnston
BUSINESS DIRECTOR: Jim Leonard

VICE PRESIDENT AND GENERAL MANAGER: Douglas J. Guendel

MEREDITH PUBLISHING GROUP

PRESIDENT: Jack Griffin
SENIOR VICE PRESIDENT: Bob Mate

MEREDITH CORPORATION

CHAIRMAN AND CHIEF EXECUTIVE OFFICER: William T. Kerr
PRESIDENT AND CHIEF OPERATING OFFICER: Stephen M. Lacy

IN MEMORIAM: E.T. Meredith III (1933-2003)

HGTV
HOME & GARDEN TELEVISION
KITCHENS

MEREDITH® BOOKS
DES MOINES, IOWA

CONTENTS

PAGE 146

PAGE 48

PAGE 129

Whether you are a gourmet cook, a take-out connoisseur, or you fall somewhere in between, there's a perfect kitchen design for you. In this hardworking section you'll learn how to store more in the space you have, easily accommodate entertaining, and beautifully light your room.

Timeless contemporary, classic European, nature-inspired beauty, and eclectic perfection—this section features these styles and more. Learn how to instill the elements of any scheme in your kitchen and coordinate the look with connecting rooms using color, accessories, and other visual cues.

Turn a cabinet front into a message board, build a table from scratch, create a custom rug, install a new faucet, tile a backsplash—learn how to tackle these projects and others with detailed step-by-step instructions and photographs.

What nitty-gritty details do you need to tend to before starting your project? Will a granite countertop fit in your budget? How much does a warming drawer cost? In this section you'll find the answers to these questions—and dozens more—regarding kitchen planning. As an added bonus this section also includes a room arranging kit, so planning your dream kitchen is a snap.

INTRODUCTION

PAGE 81

Like the programs on HGTV, this information-packed guide takes the guesswork out of restyling your kitchen. Whether you are building a new home and seek inspiration for your kitchen or you are remodeling or redecorating an existing space, *HGTV Kitchens* is your all-in-one resource for expert advice, ideas, and planning strategies to create the right room for the way you live.

HGTV Kitchens will take you through the process of creating the kitchen of your dreams. This book will help guide you from selecting the most efficient plan for your lifestyle and determining a decorating style to choosing surfaces (including flooring, countertops, and backsplashes) and calculating what it will cost to make it all happen. All the while you will learn about the latest products and appliances, materials, and design strategies from top-notch designers featured on HGTV as well as interior designers, architects, and master builders from across the country. Lush photographs of new and remodeled kitchens—including some amazing before and after transformations—decorated in myriad styles will inspire you.

   If you are eager to do some of the work yourself, don't miss the special projects section, which shows you how to tackle a wide range of kitchen improvements. You will learn how to make your own kitchen island from an old dresser, install a new faucet, and create such easy-to-achieve decorating touches as updating a backsplash and making a linoleum rug.

This book is divided into these inspiring sections:

A KITCHEN FOR EVERY NEED

Most kitchens are composed of similar pieces—a sink, a stove, a refrigerator—but different kitchens serve varying needs. If you entertain frequently you may require a different layout or amenities than if you typically dine alone. And if you cook for every meal you may need particular appliances that aren't necessary if you rely on takeout. This section shows you a multitude of kitchens that serve various functions, including kitchens tailored for cooks, those that represent command-central for all household activities (for instance bill paying and home computing), and those incorporating accessibility features. Regardless of your needs you are sure to find the right kitchen design for your lifestyle. Floor plans and planning guidelines for each space are also included, so tailoring your kitchen will be easy and efficient.

A KITCHEN FOR EVERY STYLE

Close your eyes and envision the kitchen of your dreams. Are there cabinets with fine furniture details and eloquent archways? Do sleek stainless-steel appliances and high-tech lighting components make your heart sing? Regardless of what style you desire—traditional, contemporary, cottage, or anything in between—this collection of kitchens is sure to inspire you. You will learn all about the surfaces and materials that complement each style and get expert advice on achieving the perfect style for your kitchen.

PROJECTS FOR YOUR KITCHEN

Caught the do-it-yourself bug? You're in luck: Here are 10 great projects to transform your kitchen from blah to beautiful! You'll find easy flooring solutions, simple furniture-making projects, and super decorating ideas. Additional easy-to-create projects are also sprinkled throughout the book, making this the ultimate planning and do-it-yourself guide.

PLANNING GUIDE AND ARRANGING KIT

This important section will take you through the process of creating a budget for your new or remodeled kitchen and help you select kitchen components using an easy-to-read chart. Price ranges for surfaces, appliances, and fixtures are also provided. And when you are ready to start your kitchen makeover, the planning kit will allow you to design your dream kitchen—before you enlist the help of a professional.

CREDITS AND RESOURCES

Designer contact information and resource listings for many of the products shown in the featured kitchens are provided in this section. A comprehensive index follows so you can quickly find the topics you are looking for.

Whether you want to accessorize the room you have, update your tract-home kitchen, or gut the room and start over, this collection of astounding makeovers and beautiful new spaces will whet your appetite for change and encourage you to get started. Every room is real, and the design choices and decisions are common to many homes. This is a book you will turn to again and again for practical advice and a plethora of information to make your kitchen the perfect fit for your family.

PAGE 161

PAGE 17

PAGE 67

From making a rolling island *above left* and outfitting your pantry *above* to choosing the right surfaces and fixtures *left* to complement your lifestyle, HGTV has your kitchen decisions covered. Turn the page to begin an armchair tour of some of HGTV's most inspiring kitchens.

A **KITCHEN** FOR EVERY **NEED**

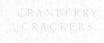

Cookie cutters certainly belong in the kitchen, but they have no place serving as inspiration for planning the functional aspects of your kitchen. Browse this section and you'll see how efficiency can be as individualized as your fingerprint. Then write down all the activities that commonly occur in your kitchen and consider what might be hampering your work or play. Also think about what new hobbies or happenings could take place if you incorporated the features to meet those needs. Of course don't forget a spot to store the cookie cutters!

HEART OF
THE HOME

A kitchen can pump life into your home—especially
when it works hard to meet everyone's needs.

Located in the center of the
house, this generous dining
area, which includes a corner
desk, is open to the kitchen
and family room.

Whether the owner wants to print photos on the computer, pay bills, plan meals, make phone calls, or work at home, this desk *right* offers enough work surface and storage to meet a variety of needs.

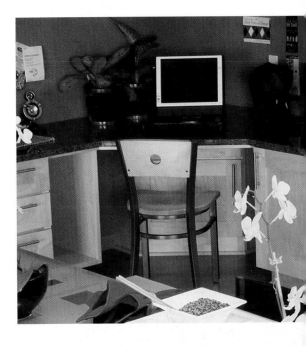

THE DAY MAY BE COMING when formal dining rooms become relics. Today many homeowners discover that sequestering this space means it goes unused—sometimes for months. For better use and efficiency merge the square footage into the kitchen, expanding your space for everyday activities—from homework to hobbies. Follow the lead of this heart-of-the-home kitchen.

MULTIPURPOSE PLANNING

The practical design *opposite* responds to the trend away from formal dining rooms, combining dining, desk work, and kitchen duty into one cohesive package. Thoughtful planning and special features make it possible to use this multipurpose space throughout the day.

The extra-large dining area, for example, works for family meals and accommodates a crowd with enough floor space for a generous-size table (or two smaller tables) to seat 12 or more. Include a built-in hutch as this design does (see the floor plan on page 15) and you'll have a handy location for storing dishes, glasses, flatware, and linens—all within easy reach of the table and the kitchen. You'll also appreciate the convenience of a dining area that opens to the kitchen. This configuration makes it easy to converse with the cook, to transport food, and to clean up after dinner. Connect these spaces with a family room and include a long window seat as this space does, and family and guests will have room to relax before and after meals.

Incorporating a raised countertop ledge between the kitchen and dining area, as shown *opposite,* provides another place to sit and chat, eat a snack, or spread out food and tableware for a buffet-style meal.

A 24-inch-deep countertop for the snack bar—instead of the typical 14 inches—*above* allows plenty of space for multiple dishes and trays of food for entertaining buffet style. The countertop is higher than the sink surface to screen kitchen messes from view.

Located between the range and refrigerator (see the floor plan *opposite above*), the warming drawer doesn't require much space but offers convenience at meal times. This allows you to make side dishes ahead of time and use the drawer to keep the food the right temperature—without drying out—while you prepare the main dish.

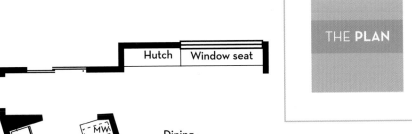

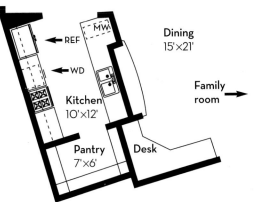

Hutch | Window seat

REF ←
MW
WD ←

Dining
15'×21'

Family
room →

Kitchen
10'×12'

Pantry
7'×6'

Desk

Even when it isn't time for a meal, a dining area can remain useful when you position a desk in one corner. The desk, shown on page 13, includes a generous work surface as well as drawers, cabinets, and cubbies for plenty of storage.

WORK CORE WONDER

Smart planning yields efficiency in the kitchen too. Choose a galley-style layout similar to this one and you'll save steps and minimize cleaning chores. But don't let the modest 10×12-foot dimensions of the space deceive you: The work core is fully equipped with a range, refrigerator, dishwasher, microwave oven, and even a warming drawer. There's also enough counter space for preparing meals and room for more than one cook. The cabinets in this industrious kitchen are packed with storage features, including divided drawers and cabinets, and pullouts for spices and dual waste receptacles (see page 18 for some of these features). Even the stylishly sleek chrome bar handles have a purpose: They're wide for easy grabbing and comfortable in hand.

PANTRY PLUS

You can minimize countertop clutter and free up cabinet space in a small kitchen by augmenting the layout with a pantry. A door at one end of this kitchen leads into a walk-in pantry (shown on page 17) lined with shelves on three walls. The pantry also features a countertop and electric outlets for storing and using small appliances, such as the blender and mixer. For help planning your own pantry and for other storage ideas, turn to page 18.

BACKSPLASHES THAT WORK

MAXIMIZE THE FUNCTION of your existing or new kitchen by putting backsplashes to work. Use one or more of these four fast-installation project ideas:

1. An array of shelves and cubbyhole units is available to fit your backsplash for storing oils, vinegars, and spices within easy reach. Look for these storage pieces at home centers, in catalogs, and through online sources. Most shelves install with screws. Cubby units can rest directly on the countertop or screw to the backsplash or upper cabinets.

2. Metal storage systems, such as the chrome bar unit on the backsplash *opposite*, are available from the same sources as noted above and easily screw into place. Grid-style units with moveable metal S-hooks are another stylish option.

3. Slotted wooden and metal racks screw to the bottom of upper cabinets and stow stemware upside down.

4. Eyehooks and cup hooks screw into upper cabinets or the backsplash. Slip cup handles, pot holders, or utensils over cup hooks. Stretch wire between eyehooks and use metal clips to hold recipes, takeout menus, pot holders, and other lightweight items.

Slate tiles lend warmth to the backsplash *right*. The chrome storage bar keeps utensils and spices within easy reach.

BAMBOO BEAUTY

BAMBOO FLOORING, used throughout this kitchen and dining area, brings unusual and beautiful graining to the rooms. Though bamboo is one of the strongest, most durable, and most stable flooring products available, it isn't actually categorized as a wood—bamboo is a grass that grows at an almost unbelievable rate of 3 feet per day. The botanical fact that bamboo matures in six years and regenerates without replanting makes it an exceptionally environmentally friendly choice. The planks begin as round, hollow shoots, which are cut into strips, boiled, dried, and laminated together. Bamboo is typically available in a light coloration (achieved by bleaching at the manufacturing plant) or in a darker tone (accomplished through pressure steaming). The product installs much like traditional tongue-and-groove hardwood flooring. Expect to pay anywhere from $2 to $9 per square foot for bamboo flooring, plus the cost of installation.

Sleek chrome bar handles suit the clean, contemporary look of the light maple cabinetry.

A door at the end of the galley kitchen opens to reveal a walk-in pantry with shelves on three walls *left*. The additional counter space and outlets make this an ideal space for storing and using countertop appliances, including a food processor, blender, and stand mixer.

STELLAR STORAGE

The kitchen shown on pages 12-17 incorporates a surprising amount of storage. Here are ideas for creating a storage-smart kitchen.

PULLOUTS PLUS The kitchen on pages 12-17 features drawers with dividers *above* to keep the contents organized. A slice of space to the right of the range is ideal for this pullout shelving unit *below* to keep spices and small jars organized.

PANTRY PLANNING Ralph Haskins, the designer and builder of the kitchen shown on pages 12-17, planned the pantry (shown on page 17) to include counter space for small appliances. The pantry door closes to conceal appliances from view. When needed the appliances can be plugged in and used where they sit. To plan your pantry, follow these suggestions:

SIZE UP YOUR NEEDS

Know your personal requirements. Cooks who work mostly with fresh ingredients may want to devote less space to nonperishables. If you rely on prepared foods—especially if you buy in bulk—you'll want more storage.

Determine the ideal pantry size. Add up how much square footage you devote to pantry items now, whether they're stored in your kitchen, basement, or garage. This gives you an idea of the amount of space you'll need to consolidate items.

Fulfill several storage tasks. Walk-in pantries are popular when space allows. Use the pantry to replace other closet needs, such as storing the broom and dustpan.

Let a shallow pantry serve you. Shallow shelves make it easy to see at a glance what's on hand.

MAXIMIZE STORAGE

Make the most of vertical space. In a new or existing pantry, use adjustable shelves to stagger the heights and avoid wasted space. Racks that hang on the backs of doors or from stationary shelves also optimize storage.

Install pullout shelves. Instead of reaching to the back of deep, immobile shelves, pull shelves toward you for easier access.

Arrange items so labels are visible. Store cans one deep and on their sides in shallow drawers to easily view the labels. This also works well for spice containers, which may fall over when placed on a turntable.

MOLDED IMAGE In a baker's preparation area, plan for a drawer, such as the one *top*, with acrylic bins that hold 20 pounds each of flour and sugar. In the same area, incorporate a flip-up shelf for the mixer *above*.

DISPLAY AND STORE Even the shallow space between wall studs can be put to work. Tongue-and-groove boards provide a charming backdrop for this tray display and storage rack *above*, which is carved out between the studs. For storing trays and platters in a pantry, install suitably sized slots inside a cabinet.

EASY RECYCLING A trio of lift-out plastic baskets *right* tucks inside an extra-deep pullout compartment to make recycling easy and orderly. Plastic liners keep baskets sanitary. Locate a recycling center close to an exterior door for quick toting outside.

For more **kitchen storage ideas**, visit *HGTV.com/organized*

This mini-kitchen peninsula features a snack counter that is higher than the sink-level countertop to conceal messes from the family room, which is out of view to the left. Tall stools make this a place to gather and enjoy drinks and snacks, with additional seating at the bar-height table in the sunroom beyond.

MINI-BENEFITS

A bar or mini-kitchen may be small, but these secondary compact work cores can be superfunctional.

IF YOU LOVE TO GATHER with friends and family, a spacious kitchen designed for entertaining is practically a must. Even if your kitchen already welcomes a crowd, you can enhance the flow of the party by including a mini-kitchen elsewhere in the house. If you're not inclined to large gatherings, a second small work core offers convenience and fun for you, for two, or more.

LOCATION, LOCATION

Picture this: You're in your lower-level family room when you realize that a soda and a bag of popcorn would go great with the movie you're watching. You pause the DVD and simply walk a few steps to the mini-kitchen and get what you need.

Or consider this: You're in the main kitchen preparing dinner when your teenager comes home with a group of thirsty and hungry friends. You smile—uninterrupted— as they head to the great room where one corner of the space is dedicated to a beverage and snack bar.

The first step to creating any mini-kitchen is deciding where to put it. Turn the mini-kitchen into a popular hangout by locating it in an active gathering area, yet away

from the main kitchen. This gives guests and family an alternative destination for snacks and drinks.

"MINI" CHOICES

Mini-kitchen options include a fully equipped U-shape work core, a smaller L-shape layout as shown on page 23, or a single stretch of cabinetry. You can even tuck an upper and lower cabinet into a closet and close it off when it's not in use.

At minimum equip a mini-kitchen with a small sink, faucet, and an undercounter refrigerator, which requires running plumbing and electricity lines to the location. Depending on your needs try boosting the function of a minimally equipped bar by adding a microwave oven, an icemaker, and a dishwasher or dishwasher drawer. A second dishwasher in the house proves especially handy for cleaning up after a party or holiday dinner. You may also want a wine chiller. (For more information about wine storage, turn to pages 32–37.)

Your mini-kitchen should also include storage for dish towels, napkins, cleaners, glassware, dishware, and flatware as well as space for nonrefrigerated snacks.

Enclosed upper cabinetry is just one option for increasing storage in a bar or mini-kitchen. Open shelves such as these *above* offer a unique design opportunity and steer the look away from too-traditional while still providing ample storage and display.

CHEERS!

PART OF THE FUN of designing a bar or mini-kitchen is shopping for accessories. These champagne stems *below* resemble a bouquet when placed in a glass vase. Leave the glass bouquet on the countertop as a pretty display, or fill the flutes with your favorite vintage and toast a big event. For more ideas on how to equip a mini-kitchen or bar, see pages 24-25.

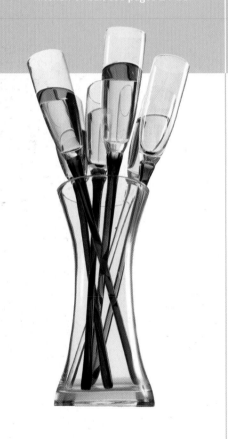

SIZE VERSUS SIZZLE

While mini-kitchens are modest in size compared to most main kitchens, they can be big on style. When decorating your mini-kitchen, feel free to use the same great surfaces and finishes that you would in a traditional kitchen. Choose cabinetry and countertop materials to suit your budget as well as the style of the adjoining spaces. Because you are equipping and decorating a smaller space, you may be able to splurge on a few higher-price materials or components, such as granite countertops and a dishwasher drawer, and still remain on-budget. This lower-level mini-kitchen *opposite* is open to a family room and a sunroom. Apple green color walls enhance sunlight and show off sleek granite countertops and light maple cabinets. The angled peninsula and custom shelves serve as architectural bonuses. Accessories on the open shelves provide beauty and function. Stainless-steel and chrome elements inject shine. For more ideas on equipping a mini-kitchen, turn the page.

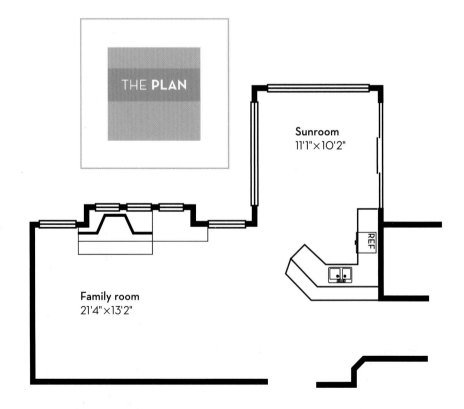

THE **PLAN**

Sunroom
11'1"×10'2"

REF

Family room
21'4"×13'2"

The floor tile in this lower-level mini-kitchen and the stain-resistant carpet in the adjoining family room (see the floor plan *opposite*) can handle food and beverage spills. The stainless-steel undercounter refrigerator balances the warm wooden cabinets with polished shine, while the angled peninsula adds architectural interest.

23

EQUIP A MINI-KITCHEN

To equip a mini-kitchen as functional and attractive as the one shown on pages 20–23, look for components, materials, and accessories at home centers, discount stores, bookstores, and online.

GOOD READS Prepare everything from nonalcoholic smoothies to martinis and other drinks using an assortment of beverage-making guides *above*. Include open shelves in your mini-kitchen so you have space to house your new collection near the blender and bar sink.

SHAKE UP To make mixed drinks like a pro, have commonly used bar tools on hand, such as a martini shaker *below*. This shaker features a revolving stainless-steel exterior cylinder with cutouts that reveal the ingredients of drink recipes.

CLEAN START If you're designing a mini-kitchen, equip the countertop with a full-size sink. For smaller work centers consider a small bar sink *above* that's just right for rinsing glasses and fixing drinks.

QUICK FIX A microwave oven *above* is a handy appliance to include in your mini-kitchen for heating leftovers, warming frozen dinners, and popping popcorn. For more complete cooking needs, such as baking ready-to-heat cookies, purchase a combination convection/microwave oven.

POWER DRAWERS A variety of appliances now comes in space-saving models, such as this refrigerator drawer *left*. Freezer drawers and dishwasher drawers are also available.

Two sinks and a professional-style stainless-steel cooktop equipped with a vegetable and pasta steamer make this kitchen efficient enough to host cooking classes (something the owner has done on several occasions).

STREAMLINED COOKING

A smooth, unobtrusive design makes cooking the center of attention in this minimalistic kitchen.

Two large appliance garages *right* keep small appliances and coffee service under wraps—and reduce countertop clutter.

THIS SLEEK, industrial-looking kitchen, designed by Chris Tosdevin and featured on HGTV's series *Kitchen Trends 2005*, is designed to make food preparation, cooking, and cleanup as efficient and stress-free as possible. To create the same feel and functionality in your kitchen, opt for clean lines and smooth, industrial-strength surfaces. This pared-down look not only makes it easier to cook, but the soothing environment also helps everyone who gathers in the space feel relaxed.

COOKS' KITCHEN

The first step in achieving a hardworking kitchen similar to this one is to choose a layout that best matches your cooking style. (To review some highly functional kitchen layouts, see page 30.) As shown in the floor plan on page 28, the large L-shape work core in this kitchen provides enough counter space for multiple cooks. A pair of sinks—one in the island and one along the long leg of the L—enables cooks to work back-to-back without getting in each other's way. On the short leg of the L, a five-burner cooktop and steamer provide ample cooking power. A partial wall opposite the island houses two combination convection- and conventional-heat ovens, a warming drawer, a refrigerator, and a food pantry. A microwave oven, coffeemaker, and other small appliances are located in the pair of appliance garages next to the sink window. (For more information on work triangles and work center design, see pages 68–69.)

STREAMLINED CABINETS

After you have a clear vision of what layout will work best for your needs, choose cabinets that are equally as hardworking. For a clean-lined look, choose flat-front cabinets in a light, subtly grained wood, such as ash, birch, or maple, or with solid-color laminate fronts. For a fresh take on cabinetry, choose cabinets in two different colors. Here pale gray-color laminate covers the cabinets on the island and the L-shape perimeter, while dark graphite-color linoleum covers the cabinets fitted along the partial wall. For extra interest both cabinet finishes are accented with aluminum edge bands and long

Narrow base cabinets on the opposite side of the island provide storage for baking supplies. Engineered quartz counters *above* are as smooth and cool as marble and resist stains.

CABINET FINISHES

THIS KITCHEN successfully mixes two types of laminated cabinetry finishes to create a sophisticated look with a wipe-clean finish. Here's a rundown on the most common cabinet finishes:

WOOD Most cabinets are covered in a combination of solid wood pieces and wood veneers. Before you select a wood for your cabinets, consider the grain pattern and durability of a given species. All woods can be treated with a variety of stains and top coats to achieve different looks and greater durability. The range of appearances varies greatly in some species, and different pieces of the same wood may take stain differently, so be sure and look at a variety of cabinet samples before making your final finish decision. If the wood you like best is out of your price range, ask your cabinet dealer about compromises. Maple stained to resemble cherry will give you a look close to actual cherry, but it won't cost as much. (For cabinetry pricing information, see pages 176 and 179.)

LAMINATES High-pressure laminates, as shown on the pale gray-color cabinets on page 26, are made from durable and stain-resistant plastic resins available in a wide range of colors. Low-pressure laminates, often found on inexpensive shelves and closet organizers, may chip. Linoleum laminates, as shown on the graphite-color cabinets *opposite*, are not as common as the other varieties but are nearly as durable; like the flooring, linoleum laminates are made from renewable resources.

VINYL FILMS Also known as thermo-foil films, vinyl films are heat-laminated to a medium-density fiberboard (MDF) backing. Although vinyl film resembles a painted wood finish, the material is impervious to water and can be wiped down with a damp cloth. The kitchen on pages 86–93 features cabinets with a thermo-foil finish.

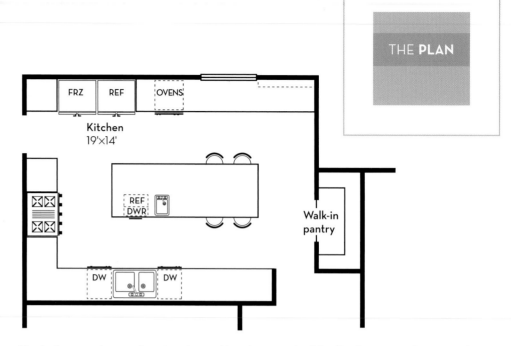

The L-shape work core *above* is enhanced by a large center island and storage cabinets on the opposite side of the island. Refrigerator drawers hidden in the island make it the perfect place for storing and preparing fresh fruits and vegetables. Additional appliances include two combination conventional/convection ovens, a warming drawer, a microwave, and two dishwashers that flank the main sink. A commercial-grade refrigerator and freezer are located adjacent to the ovens.

stainless-steel handles. (For more information on cabinet materials, see "Cabinet Finishes" *left.*)

OPTIONS FOR INDUSTRIAL-STRENGTH COUNTERTOPS

The engineered quartz counters featured in this kitchen are a perfect complement to industrial style because of their clean look and incredible strength. Made from crushed quartz and binders, the material has a composition, weight, and price comparable to granite. Because it is nonporous, the material doesn't require sealants and is ideal for use in moisture-prone areas. If this material doesn't suit

you, there are other options that also work well in a sleek kitchen, including concrete, stainless steel, and nonporous stone.

Concrete counters are nearly as durable as granite, and the surface stands up to hot-off-the-stove pans. To prevent stains seal concrete once or twice a year.

Stainless-steel counters are affordably priced and heat-resistant. They also allow for one-piece countertop/sink formations. Note that this surface does show spots and fingerprints and can be scratched by abrasive cleaners and sharp knives.

Like concrete and engineered quartz, stone counters stand up to heat, water, and knives and are excellent for rolling out dough. For maintenance-free service choose a nonporous stone like granite. For a minimalistic look select a solid-color stone in a honed finish; shiny finishes tend to show fingerprints. (For countertop pricing guidelines, see page 180.)

EASY-CARE FLOORS

Wood, laminate, ceramic tile, and stone all make for easy-care floors that look great in a streamlined kitchen. Hardwoods, as shown in this kitchen, are available with a prefinished or site-applied urethane coating that tolerates kitchen traffic without denting or scratching. Laminate floors offer the look of wood, tile, or stone at a slightly lower price than the real things and stand up equally well to kitchen traffic. Durable and resistant to moisture, ceramic tiles are a common choice for contemporary kitchens and wipe clean with a damp mop. Stone floors also require little maintenance; however, more porous varieties such as marble and limestone may require sealing to prevent staining. To disguise fingerprints and dust on any of these hard surfaces, choose a honed finish.

MORE PLANNING OPTIONS

To see floor plans for four additional hardworking, streamlined kitchens, turn the page.

With the exception of the wall ovens and cooktops, the appliances in this kitchen hide behind cabinetry panels. A commercial-grade refrigerator and freezer are located adjacent to the ovens. Stainless-steel handles and aluminum accents on the cabinetry complement the focal-point range and match the high-tech styling of the room.

CLUTTER BUSTERS To keep the counters clear of clutter, store small appliances in easy-to-access garages and kitchen gear behind closed doors. To maximize the capacity and increase the organization within your cabinets, install storage organizers such as below-the-shelf and inside-the-door hanging baskets; both will keep smaller items neat and within reach. Cabinet organizers are available at home centers and closet organizing stores.

STREAMLINED LAYOUTS

The layout of the kitchen featured on pages 26–29 enables two or more cooks to work together. Review these four basic arrangements to see if one of them better suits the way you and your family use your kitchen space.

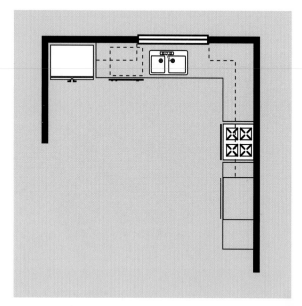

L-SHAPE The most island-friendly configuration, the L-shape kitchen *above* requires the least amount of space and offers the most flexibility. In this setup two workstations are situated on one wall, and a third is placed on an adjacent wall. Location of the workstations is paramount: Work should flow from the refrigerator to the sink and then to the cooktop and serving area. If you plan to include an island, move either the sink or the cooktop to the island top to streamline the workflow.

U-SHAPE This configuration *below* includes one workstation on each of three walls and works well for one cook. A space of at least 8×8 feet is needed for a U-shape kitchen to provide at least 4 feet of work space in the center of the room. You can modify this arrangement by making one of the sidewalls a half-wall for an open connection to the great room.

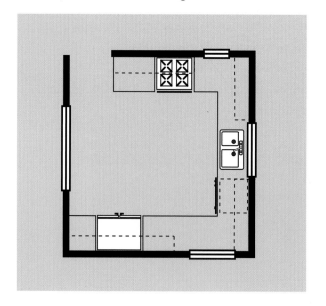

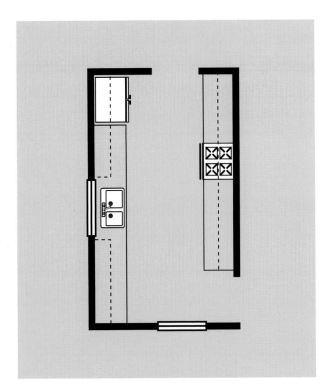

GALLEY This setup *above* fits a kitchen that serves as a corridor between two rooms. With a center aisle measuring at least 4 feet wide, parallel walls allow the cook to move easily from one workstation to another. The wide aisle also keeps traffic out of the cook's way. Housing the sink and refrigerator on one wall with the cooktop centered on the other wall maximizes efficiency.

DUAL WORKSTATION This arrangement *below* works great for multiple cooks and lots of visitor traffic. An island with a second sink creates a companion area to the traditional work triangle of the refrigerator, cooktop, and main sink. A second work zone also can become a snack center for a family on the go. Accessorize the counter with stools and a microwave oven for quick and easy meals.

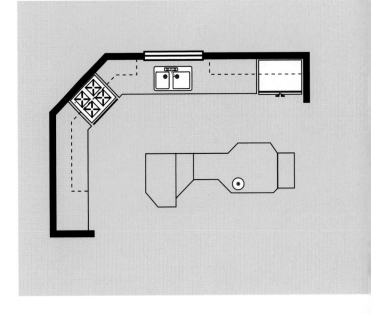

Locate a bar right outside your wine cellar for convenience and to welcome more guests. This granite-topped bar (with a view into the wine cellar) includes a sink and faucet on the lower countertop level (out of camera view) and enough space around the upper ledge for a group of six.

WINE CELLAR SAVOIR FAIRE

Discover the convenience and pleasures of having well-designed wine storage at home.

IF YOU'RE BUILDING a new home, it's easy to designate one room within your floor plan as a wine cellar. In an existing home, space for a wine cellar can easily be claimed and retrofitted. While the wine cellar shown *opposite* is located off a basement-level recreation room in a new house, you can establish a wine room on any level of a new or existing home. An unused bedroom or even a large closet, for example, can be equipped for stocking and preserving wines.

WINE CELLAR BASICS

The goal is to create storage space that provides a stable, optimal environment for preserving wine and allowing it to mature at the proper rate. Consider these basic requirements for an in-home wine cellar:

Temperature. Both red and white wines store well in temperatures ranging from 50 to 55 degrees Fahrenheit. The key is to avoid wide fluctuations in temperature, which damage the wine. Cooling units designed for wine cellars start at about $1,000 for small models with no humidifying features to $14,000 for deluxe refrigeration systems equipped with waterfalls for increasing the level of humidity.

Humidity. Maintaining a humidity level of about 70 percent is ideal for storing wine because the added moisture prevents the corks from drying out and shrinking. A shrunken cork allows oxygen into the bottle, prematurely aging the contents and eventually turning the wine to vinegar.

Insulation. To retain cooled and humidified air inside your wine cellar, the walls, ceiling, and floor require a vapor barrier and insulation. Use fiberglass batts or polystyrene board insulation between studs and joists—at least R-13 insulation for walls and R-19 for the ceiling. One way to insulate a basement-level cement floor is to cover the floor with a plastic vapor barrier, top the vapor barrier with a series of 2×2s, and fill the spaces between the boards with polystyrene board. Top the 2×2s and insulation with plywood and finish the floor as desired.

Vapor barrier. To prevent condensation from migrating into the insulation, install a vapor barrier on the warm side. Some insulation comes with a vapor barrier attached; if not, use plastic sheeting as a vapor barrier.

Doorway. To keep the conditioned air inside your wine cellar, provide access into the interior with an exterior-quality door equipped with weatherstripping and a threshold.

Storage. Check local wine specialty stores, wine supply catalogs, and online sources for a variety of wine rack solutions. Purchase racks made of metal, cement, or woods, such as redwood, oak, or mahogany, that stand up well to the humid environment without special sealers or finishes. The wood you choose also shouldn't emit an odor; for example avoid cedar because the odor can migrate through the cork and taint the flavor of the wine. No matter what type of racking system you purchase, always store wine on its side so the content remains in contact with the cork to prevent the cork from drying out, shrinking, and allowing oxygen into the bottle.

Cultured-stone walls and wood ceiling planks create a dynamic setting for enjoying a glass of wine at the table for two. Wood racks tucked into the arched niches make it possible to preserve and age 550 bottles of wine.

BLENDING ATMOSPHERE AND PRACTICALITY

NEW HOME BUILDER Jim Harmeyer of Tyler Homes included this wine cellar (see the floor plan *below*) in the lower level of a show house as part of a recreation room. "People love the idea of being able to collect and store wine in their own home, so we have begun to include these spaces more than ever before," he says.

Jim wanted the entire house to have an old-world feel (to view the old-world style kitchen in this same house, turn to page 100). "We finished the room with a combination of cultured-stone walls and wood on the ceiling," Jim says. Porcelain floor tiles—with chattered edges—enhance the aged look. The wine cellar is spacious enough to accommodate a bar-height table for two at the center of the room—a feature that is as romantic as it is functional.

A key to successfully storing wine is keeping the bottles in the dark most of the time because light ages wine more quickly. (That's why wine never comes in clear bottles.) Still a wine cellar needs lighting so you can find what you want. In this cellar lighting fixtures are on dimmers so illumination levels can be set on high when searching for wine or adjusted lower to create a tranquil atmosphere for enjoying a glass of wine at the table. Install only halogen and/or incandescent fixtures in your wine cellar; fluorescent lighting emits UV (ultraviolet) light, which can prematurely age wine.

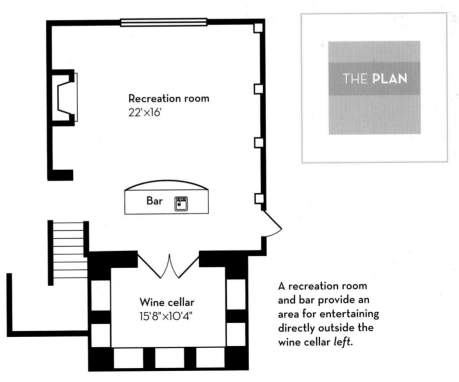

Recreation room
22'×16'

THE **PLAN**

Bar

Wine cellar
15'8"×10'4"

A recreation room and bar provide an area for entertaining directly outside the wine cellar *left*.

WINE READY

Shop around and you'll discover an abundance of products to help you enjoy collecting wines at home.

CHARMING IDEA So whose glass is whose? Clip a different wine glass charm *below* to the stem of each glass and you'll never play that guessing game again.

Glass duos. You can drink white wine out of any type of glass, but if you want to follow convention, purchase more slender, cone-shaped glasses for white wine *below* and larger, more bulbous glasses for red.

Theme scheme. Play up the wine theme at your bar or inside the wine cellar with art and other accessories sporting pertinent motifs, such as wine bottle-emblazoned bar towels.

READ ALL ABOUT IT Learn more about wine collecting and storage with these books: *The World Atlas of Wine* by Hugh Johnson and Jancis Robinson *above; How and Why to Build a Wine Cellar* by Richard M. Gold, Ph.D.; *Collecting Wine: You and Your Cellar* by James Halliday; and *Cellaring Wine: Managing Your Wine Collection ... to Perfection* by Jeff Cox and William Bramhall.

WAYS TO STORE WINE

ON THE RACK. If you don't need to store wine for months or years, it's acceptable to store bottles in your kitchen on an open rack. Locate the rack away from sources of heat and direct light and use the wine as soon as possible. Place bottles in the racks with the wine labels facing up so you can see what type and vintage they are without disturbing the bottles. Wine matures best with minimal movement. To make it easier to find wines, divide your collection between red and white. Further divide the categories as desired, such as by vintage.

START A JOURNAL. Record your inventory, noting the type of wine, vintage, cost, and where you bought it. Every once in a while, open a bottle from one case to see if it has reached its prime. Note the results in your journal and be specific about the taste; you'll appreciate the notations in the future when you go on your next buying trip.

IN THE CLOSET. Insulate a kitchen closet, add a small cooler, and convert the space into a tall wine chiller. While a glass door won't hold cool air and humidity in as well as a solid door, most connoisseurs like to keep their collection on display.

UNDER THE COUNTER. Wine chillers come in a variety of sizes and models. Many units fit under the counter and hold about 24 bottles.

COOL THINKING Get the party started with an ice bucket to keep bottles nicely chilled. This acrylic version *right* puts the beauty of the labels on display and lets you see right away when the supply runs low. For more intimate gatherings, a stainless-steel bucket *above* can keep one bottle of wine nearby and table ready.

Opening and closing statements. Most wines still come sealed with a cork, so purchase a good-quality corkscrew for opening. If you won't consume the entire bottle in a few hours, seal it with a bottle plug. A variety of bottle plugs is available at your local wine shop.

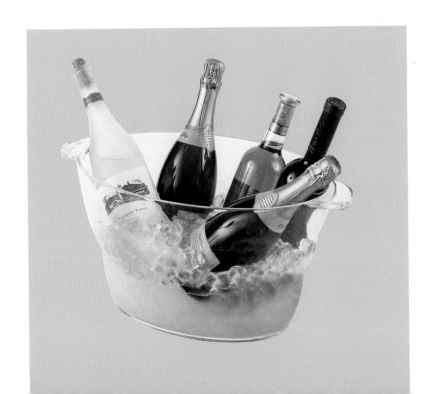

EASY ENTERTAINING

You'll love the functionality that a kitchen designed for entertaining brings to your home.

This warm and inviting kitchen beckons guests to come in and enjoy the hospitality. A wall of windows provides every guest with a spectacular view of the colorful backyard garden and tree-lined property.

KITCHENS ARE AT THE HEART of every home. They're natural gathering spaces for family and friends where you come together for food and fellowship. In fact, according to recent studies, people spend more waking hours in the kitchen than any other room of the home. If you frequently entertain, look to this kitchen for innovative design strategies and decorating ideas that will ensure every event you host is a social success. And even if you don't host weekly gatherings, the ideas featured here will make daily cooking and eating more enjoyable.

CROWD CAPACITY

An open layout (see the floor plan on page 45) allows guests to flow comfortably from

Red-painted cabinet interiors and dentil molding painted in the same color bring a touch of warmth to the creamy-white cabinets *above*. The owners painted these details using household paint and artist's brushes after the cabinets were installed.

CUSTOMIZE WITH COLOR Give the interiors of your glass-fronted cabinets a custom look by painting them a contrasting color. If you have more time, paint decorative moldings the same color as the cabinet interior as shown *above*. Mask off adjoining cabinets and use small artist's brushes to fill in details.

A hand-painted table and comfy leather chairs encourage guests to sit and relax. Warm honey-tone floors create comfort underfoot.

When closed this dishwasher drawer *right* and *below* looks like any other storage drawer in the kitchen. It offers enough capacity for daily dishes. The full-size washer on the opposite side of the sink accommodates cleanup after entertaining a crowd. Solid surfacing covers the perimeter countertops.

the kitchen to the dining room, family room, or to a patio or garden. Similarly a large center island, such as the L-shape workhorse shown on page 38, provides enough work space for several cooks and guests to gather. Generous aisles allow plenty of room to mingle. If you have the space, bump the width of your island to 48 inches to provide comfortable access for guests in wheelchairs and to ensure continued accessibility for family members and friends throughout all stages of life. Facing the cooktop and a prep sink toward the family area enables the cooks to always be a part of the party.

To generate enough oven capacity to cook for a crowd, include at least two conventional ovens, a microwave, and a warming drawer.

In this kitchen a combination conventional/convection oven is located next to the refrigerator, and a second conventional oven is a few steps away in the short leg of the island. A microwave fits above the combination oven, and a warming drawer tucks below it, making it easy to keep large quantities of food at the proper temperature for serving. As another consideration for possible future needs, the combination oven opens from the side so it can be reached from either a standing or sitting position. (For more ways to make your kitchen universally accessible, see pages 56–61.)

To increase the cleanup capacity of a kitchen, include two dishwashers and two sinks. Here a drawer-size washer, shown

41

Stainless-steel appliances complement the classic French country decor without overpowering it. These stacked ovens *right* provide microwave, convection, and conventional cooking power as well as a drawer to keep snacks and desserts warm.

Decorating details are as important in this shared space as they are in any other gathering area, such as a living or family room. These bud vases *above* hold flowers picked from the nearby garden.

on page 41, located to the right of the largest sink provides enough wash space for daily dishes generated by the empty nesters. A full-size model to the left provides service for larger events. If space allows include a large pantry cabinet or closet to store cooking supplies, food, and serving pieces close at hand. To keep small appliances nearby yet out of sight, include at least one appliance garage, as shown on page 38.

WELCOMING AMBIENCE

Once you have all the functional requirements of your kitchen defined, select cabinetry and work surfaces that are both attractive and practical. A rich coffee-color glaze warms creamy-white painted cabinets in this kitchen. Dentil molding, painted a deep rich red, adds a touch of dramatic color. For more contrast

Painted in lively colors, a trio of barstools *above* provides guests a spot to land while enjoying the company of the cooks. Open shelves and plate racks provide convenient storage and enable guests and family members to grab what they need without having to open a cabinet door. The open displays also increase color and texture in the kitchen, making it feel more like a gathering area than a work zone.

glass-fronted cabinet interiors are also painted red. Countertops are made from a combination of surfaces: Shiny black granite tops the island and serving buffet; solid surfacing covers the remaining perimeter counters.

To ensure a sunny attitude, draw in as much sunlight as possible. A wall of windows provides an attractive view of the backyard garden and encourages guests to flow from the kitchen to the patio. The charm of the kitchen spills over into the adjacent family room via colorful pieces upholstered in French country motifs and a complementary color scheme. For more easy entertaining ideas, turn the page.

THE **PLAN**

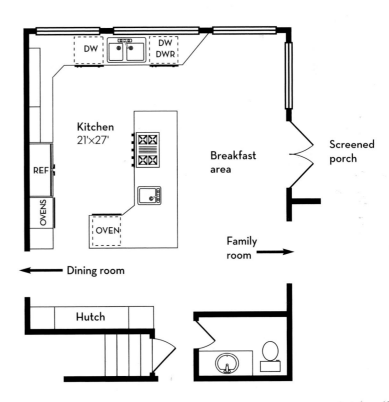

Kitchen
21'×27'

REF

OVENS

OVEN

DW

DW
DWR

Breakfast
area

Screened
porch

Family
room

← Dining room

Hutch

SOCIAL SUCCESS

As the kitchen on pages 38–45 illustrates, a kitchen designed with entertaining in mind ensures all your social gatherings garner rave reviews.

STAGING AREA When planning your kitchen, include a spot where you can serve food and drinks that does not collide with food preparation or cooking. As shown in the plan on page 45, this staging area *below* runs along the back wall of the kitchen and connects the dining room to the family room. The 6-foot-long countertop provides enough space for serving a variety of food and drinks. Glass-fronted cabinets above allow guests to help themselves to glasses or plates. Sumptuous desserts encourage guests to come back for more.

FORM MEETS FUNCTION

In addition to accommodating cooking and gathering, the best entertaining kitchens are as inviting to the eye as they are to the palate. Antique sconces, salvaged from the Orient Express *below*, provide accent and mood lighting. Made from hand-painted tile, the island sink *above* is the epitome of form meets function.

AN ENTERTAINING PLAN

THE RIGHT kitchen layout can help make any get-together a success, whether you're hosting a Super Bowl party for twenty or a dinner party for four.

AMPLE FLOOR SPACE between the center island and perimeter cabinets makes room for more than one cook and for guests who like to mingle or pitch in.

OPEN ENTRANCES to the dining room and family room and exterior doors that connect to a patio or garden encourage guests to flow from room to room.

AN EXPANSE OF WINDOWS allows for a beautiful view and fills a kitchen with an abundance of sunshine.

A FUNCTION-PACKED CENTER ISLAND provides work space for more than one cook and a place for serving buffet-style meals. Barstool seating along one side of the island enables guests to visit comfortably with the cook without being underfoot.

A COOKTOP facing an adjoining patio and family room enables cooks to be part of the conversation while putting the finishing touches on a meal.

TWO SINKS allow for two cooks to prepare food or rinse dishes at the same time.

DOUBLE OVENS provide enough baking capacity for holiday feasts or party-size desserts.

With the upper cabinets removed, the wall cabinet farthest to the right was added to increase storage. The peninsula also becomes ultrafunctional with the addition of a snack bar-height ledge and stools.

CABINET CAMPAIGN

Ready to vote out your kitchen? Relocating and replacing some cabinets can increase efficiency.

IF KITCHENS FROM THE '80s had a campaign slogan, it would probably be "Vote for Brown!" Unfortunately brown won over many homeowners, and cabinet efficiency fell by the wayside with too many wasted corners and few special storage features.

CONQUER CABINET ISSUES

Such was the case for this kitchen. Besides the overwhelming dark color of the wood, some of the cabinets were obtrusive and others practically useless. Cabinetry above the peninsula, for example, blocked the view and inhibited interaction between people in the breakfast area and anyone using the work core. The upper cabinets also rendered the peninsula (see the Before photo *right*) virtually unusable as a snack bar—a handy feature for families and for entertaining.

Corner cabinets featured interiors so deep the contents at the back became lost in the shadows. A narrow base cabinet between the range and refrigerator offered little convenience. Stacks of cookbooks cluttered the top of the refrigerator. A short antique commode, positioned beside the refrigerator, provided storage but looked awkward blocking an unused exterior door.

A BRIGHTER FUTURE

You may find any or all of these cabinet issues at your house. If so start by determining whether your cabinets can or should be saved (see "Can Your Cabinets Be Saved?" on page 51). Then use these

BEFORE

The dark-stained upper cabinets *above* worked like a wall between the breakfast area and work core in this dreary kitchen.

This kitchen *above* says goodbye to wasted corners: A lazy Susan base cabinet takes control with shelves that revolve the contents into view. An appliance garage makes best use of a corner countertop space by concealing clutter.

49

Blinds replace a flouncy valance for a clean, contemporary look that suits the new crisp colors of the cabinetry *right*. A new faucet and sink and solid-surfacing countertops team up with an embossed tile backsplash to further update the look. As a finishing flourish, the new pendant lighting fixture repeats the rich cobalt blue color of the base cabinetry.

A French door makes this pantry *left* a pretty addition to the kitchen. The glass panes help the kitchen feel more open and make it easy to see what's inside at a glance.

solutions to assure a brighter, more efficient future for your kitchen.

Eliminate. If some cabinets don't work with the new floor plan get rid of them. The owners opted to remove the upper cabinets above the peninsula in this kitchen (see page 48). (If you have a garage or basement, recycle the cabinets for workshop storage. Or donate sturdy cabinets to a local organization that builds or remodels homes for people in need.)

Add. If you're short on storage, purchase additional cabinets to meet your needs. Removing upper cabinets above the peninsula in this kitchen briefly reduced storage but opened up a spot for adding one more upper cabinet to the end of the cabinet run attached to the sink wall (see page 48). For continuity the soffit above the new cabinet was extended as well.

Trade. It's worth trading one cabinet for another when the potential convenience outweighs the temporary inconvenience of tearing out the old and installing the new. To make better use of storage space here, a cabinet equipped with a lazy Susan replaced the lower corner cabinet. Now the contents rotate into view. The new cabinet is slightly narrower, allowing room for the addition of a built-in wine rack to the left of the sink cabinet (see page 49). The upper corner cabinet was removed and

CAN YOUR CABINETS BE SAVED?

IF YOU'RE NOT SURE if your cabinets are worth saving, use this list to help you decide:

MATERIAL Take a close look at the cabinet materials. Solid-wood and metal cabinets are often worth a makeover because they can be sturdy. Cabinets constructed of particleboard or plywood might not be worth the effort because they may not hold up in the long run. If you're planning to redo metal cabinets, take them to an auto body shop for a lasting paint job.

CONSTRUCTION Inspect doors, drawers, and cabinet bodies to check for warping. Do they appear structurally sound? Wobbling and warping in the frame, shelves, or drawers indicate the cabinets likely need to be replaced.

HARDWARE How difficult would it be to replace the hinges, knobs, or pulls on your cabinets? If you plan to paint the cabinets, it's easy to fill holes used by the old knobs or pulls and to drill the fronts to accept new hardware. If you plan to add new knobs or pulls to existing stained doors, purchase decorative back plates to conceal the old holes used by the former hardware.

FINISHES Some low-quality finishes—usually applied over low-grade materials—become gooey or sticky with age and cleaning. Try stripping a spot to see if it's possible to remove the finish without damaging the veneer below. If not the cabinets aren't worth keeping. If you're dealing with multiple layers of paint but good-quality cabinets, send the doors and drawers out to be professionally stripped and use an electric palm sander to remove the paint from the cabinet boxes. (Wear a protective mask when sanding.)

THE **PLAN**

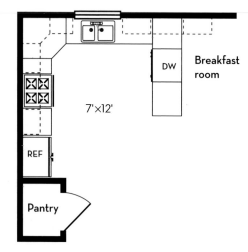

Breakfast room

DW

7'×12'

REF

Pantry

With the bank of upper cabinets removed between the work core and breakfast room, an additional cabinet was added to the run of upper cabinets on the sink wall *above*.

Gone is the clutter of books above the refrigerator. A new cabinet built around the refrigerator *above* features shelves on top for keeping the cookbook collection orderly; baskets organize small items.

replaced with a more efficient cabinet that angles across the corner (see page 55). Stepping in to replace a narrow cabinet between the range and refrigerator is a 15-inch-wide cabinet *above* offering enough extra storage and counter space to be a smart trade.

Build. The exterior door to the left of the refrigerator was never used, so the alcove becomes useful as a pantry (see page 51). The addition of an appliance garage hides clutter in the space between the upper and lower cabinets (see page 55). Wrapped in a

painted wood surround, the refrigerator *above* appears built-in and integrates visually with the surrounding cabinetry.

Paint. Brown is little more than a memory with fresh cream-color paint for the upper cabinets and a bold cobalt blue color for the base cabinets. (To learn how to paint wood cabinets, turn to page 162.)

Illuminate. Changing the lighting is one more way to freshen a kitchen. Cobalt blue pendants cast light on the peninsula and sink area (see page 48). For more tips on customizing a kitchen, turn the page.

GET THE MESSAGE To make the message board shown on the end of the peninsula (see page 54), paint the end of a cabinet (upper or lower) with three coats of magnetic paint, following the manufacturer's directions for application and drying times. Paint the end panel to match the cabinets. For more message board projects, see pages 162–163.

The table and chairs receive coats of creamy white to match the upper cabinetry.

53

CUSTOMIZE A STANDARD KITCHEN

If your cabinets are worth keeping and your kitchen layout suits your needs, incorporate some or all of these makeover lessons learned from the kitchen featured on pages 48–53.

SNACK BAR Retrofit one side of a peninsula with a taller countertop to serve as a snack bar *left*. Here a narrow frame is built onto the back side of the peninsula several inches higher than the existing countertop. Solid-surfacing material tops the snack bar, while beaded board and brackets add charm.

MESSAGE BOARD Even the end of a peninsula can become a functional kitchen feature. To learn how to make this message board *below*, turn to page 53.

SPACE SAVVY When replacing cabinets and keeping others, you'll often end up with "dead space" between cabinets. Rather than let this space go to waste, fill it with something useful, such as vertical slots for trays or a narrow rack for wine bottles as shown *below*.

LIGHTING When it's time to remodel, invest in updated lighting. Rather than use only recessed lighting, add a few pendant fixtures to bring the illumination closer to the countertop. Pendants with glass shades *above* also offer a good opportunity to splash color on the scene.

UPPER CABINET Eliminate deep, dark corners and wasted space in an upper corner cabinet by installing a standard-depth cabinet at an angle as shown *above*. Match the angle on the soffit above to lend visual continuity to the redone section.

BACKSPLASH Give the backsplash a new look without spending a bundle. This single row of embossed tiles *left* adds subtle style while providing an easy-to-clean surface. The cream color complements the solid-surfacing countertops.

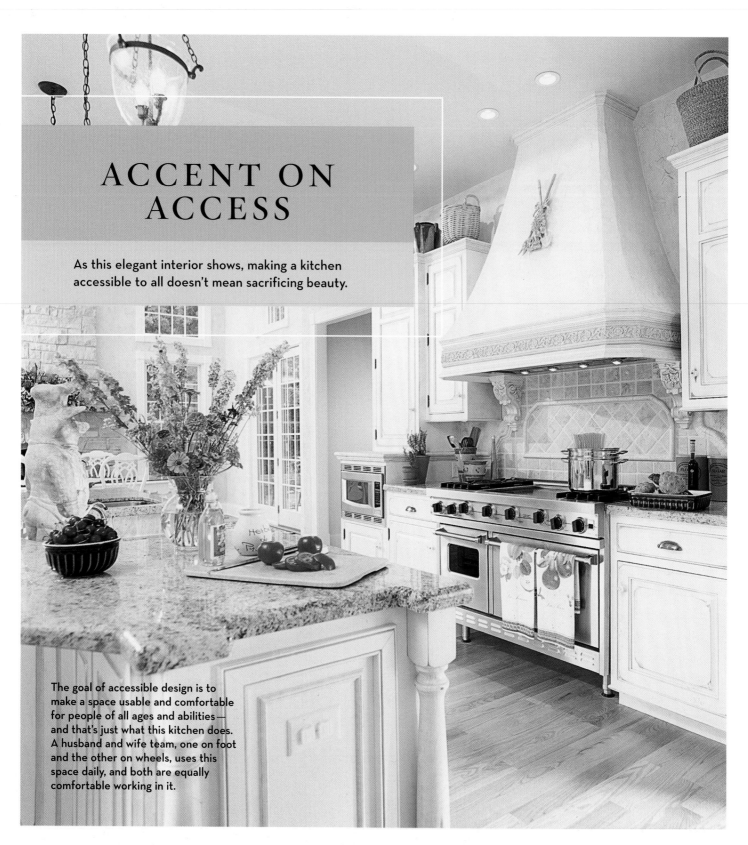

ACCENT ON ACCESS

As this elegant interior shows, making a kitchen accessible to all doesn't mean sacrificing beauty.

The goal of accessible design is to make a space usable and comfortable for people of all ages and abilities—and that's just what this kitchen does. A husband and wife team, one on foot and the other on wheels, uses this space daily, and both are equally comfortable working in it.

IF YOU'RE THE CHIEF COOK, the head bottle washer, or a late-night snacker, your kitchen can be both comfortable and stylish regardless of whether you use a wheelchair or walker now or may need to in the future. This old-world kitchen was designed for a husband and wife team, one who uses a wheelchair and one who doesn't. When designing a kitchen with accessibility in mind, make enhancements similar to those shown on the following pages to provide comfort for everyone.

OPEN SPACES

Ensuring there is ample room for wheelchair turnaround is key to an accessible space. Kitchen traffic lanes are typically about 3 feet wide, but 4-foot aisles *opposite* make maneuvering wheelchairs and walkers easier. To allow for wheelchair turnaround, plan 5 feet of clear aisle space. Allow plenty of counter space next to the refrigerator, ovens, sinks, and the cooktop to rest hot and cold items. People using wheelchairs and walkers need one hand free to steer, which makes it difficult to carry more than one object at a time. The landing areas also provide work space where you need it.

ACCOMMODATING APPLIANCES

Numerous appliances currently on the market offer ease of use to people of all ages and abilities. Wall ovens with side-hinged doors (see the kitchen

The fully integrated style of this dishwasher *above*, with controls in the upper door rim, allows the appliance to blend with the cabinetry—and the hidden buttons can't be accidentally pushed in. Granite counters and distressed cabinets set a stylish Tuscan tone. Old-fashioned cup-style pulls make it easy to open drawers, even when mobility is limited.

THE PLAN

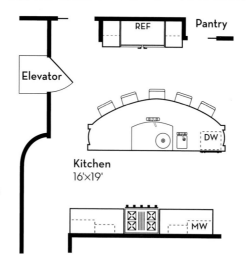

Pantry

REF

Elevator

Kitchen
16'×19'

DW

MW

ROLLING PLAN The refrigerator and "roll-in" pantry are positioned to make putting away groceries easy. Wide aisles around the large center island *right* enable two cooks to work together without running into each other.

on page 43 for this feature) and a separate cooktop with knee space below allow the cook convenient access. The chef in this kitchen opted for a professional-style range because of its precision cooking capabilities and its accessible front controls. To reduce the possibility of burns, the wheeling chef uses only the front burners and reserves the back burners for his comrade. Another idea: Position the microwave low enough so it can be reached from a sitting position, but high enough so it doesn't open into knees or armrests. The microwave in this kitchen, shown on page 61, tucks below a 48-inch-high counter.

Under-the-counter refrigerator and freezer drawers accommodate users of all abilities. Side-by-side refrigerators *opposite* are another option; most of the storage

drawers and bins are accessible to everyone regardless of height. When planning sink heights think multilevel: Install one at the standard 36-inch height for standers and one 5 or 6 inches lower for sitters as shown in this kitchen on page 57. To prevent hot pipes from burning bare legs, move all water supply lines to the back of the sink.

FRIENDLY FINISHES

Layout and appliances aren't the only considerations to keep in mind when planning a kitchen with accessible features: Select eye-catching surfaces and finishes that are also durable and ensure safety for users. Choose classic cabinetry with a distressed finish, such as the furniture-quality painted cherry wood cabinets used in this kitchen, so dings from a bumping wheelchair won't detract

from the finish and may actually add more character. Richly stained, prefinished hardwood floors are firm and smooth under feet and wheels, making them a good choice for any kitchen. Tile is another option, but grout joints need to be even with the tile surface, not below—otherwise every bump may be felt. Vinyl is also a suitable flooring option, but choose a high-quality variety that can withstand the wear of wheels. Opt for an ever-stylish bullnose shape for countertop edges to give arms a comfortable spot to rest and to prevent denting and bruising, which sharper, square edges can cause.

ACCESSIBLE STORAGE

Meld beauty and functionality by including open cubbies in the island. Store everyday items, such as dishes, pots, and pans, in base cabinets equipped with roll-out drawers that reduce the need to reach. To increase the storage capacity of all shelves and make units jut out farther for easier access, install wall cabinets that are 15 to 18 inches deep instead of the typical 12 inches. And rather than equipping a walk-in or roll-in pantry closet with a swinging door, choose a pocket door that slides into the wall to allow a wheelchair to enter and exit easily. For more ways to increase accessibility, turn the page.

The extra-wide aisles and smooth hardwood floors in this kitchen maximize accessibility and accentuate the spaciousness of the bright room.

ACCESSIBLE DESIGN

Whether your friends and family walk or roll, make them feel comfortable and welcome by including a few of the accessible design features gleaned from the kitchen on pages 56–59 in your own space.

SIDE-BY-SIDE SINKS Two sinks, one designed for roll-up service and the other for walk-up, make preparing food and cleaning up comfortable for both walkers and rollers.

DETAILS, DETAILS Wire inserts on the cabinet drawers beside the refrigerator provide storage for items that require airflow. The inserts are durable enough to withstand a bump or two from a wheelchair or walker.

EASY-ACCESS MICROWAVE Tucked below a 48-inch-high counter, this microwave is convenient to use whether the person is standing or sitting. Create similar comfort by placing the appliance on a standard countertop or a microwave cart.

NUMBERS TO KNOW

THE NATIONAL KITCHEN and Bath Association (NKBA) recommends these guidelines when planning an accessible kitchen.

COMFORTABLE REACH Locate door handles, appliances, electrical outlets, and switches 15 to 48 inches above the floor so anyone can reach them comfortably.

AISLE AND APPROACH ROOM Aisles that are 4 feet wide comfortably accommodate wheelchairs and are recommended for multi-cook kitchens. Plan 5 feet of clear space for wheelchair turnarounds. Ideally there should be two turnarounds in the kitchen: one near the refrigerator and one near the cooktop or sink.

KNEE CLEARANCES, TOE-KICKS Wheelchair users require knee clearances that are 27 inches high, 30 inches wide, and 19 inches deep. Similarly extra-wide toe-kicks allow chair users to pull up close to counters. Some cabinet manufacturers offer these wide toe-kicks as an option; other cabinets may be modified.

FAUCETS AND HOT WATER Hands-free faucets that turn on with a sensor reduce the necessity to reach. Single-handle lever faucets as shown in the lower sink *opposite left* are easier to turn on and off than two-handle varieties. To prevent scalding turn your hot water down to 120 degrees.

DOORS AND HANDLES Plan for a clear door opening of 36 inches. Equip entrance doors, cabinet doors, and drawers with lever or cup handles, which are easier to operate than knobs.

WINDOWS Casement windows are the easiest to operate from a sitting position. Install windows 24 to 30 inches above the floor so wheelchair users can open, close, and easily see out of them.

Opening your kitchen to other areas of the house can free up space for a larger work core and increase function with more cabinetry. In this kitchen, removing half-walls between the kitchen and breakfast area accommodates a work core that's centered around a large multipurpose island. The window at the end of the room was reduced to half its original height to make room for more cabinetry and a countertop.

HIDDEN ASSETS

The best cabinetry boasts both beauty and brains, as this kitchen illustrates with its well-crafted storage.

TEENAGE GIRLS ARE PRETTY in pink, but apply this powdery shade to a tiled kitchen countertop and you may feel like you've stepped back into the 1950s. This kitchen *below* definitely stirred up visions of a dated decor, but worse than that the cabinets started falling apart and the tiles began popping off the countertops, making the space difficult to work in.

You may be facing the same decade-defying dilemma at your house, and though you might be fond of the '50s, you probably don't want to cook there. To remedy an unintended retro look and failing cabinets and countertops, use this dynamic kitchen, featured on *Designers' Challenge,* as a guide for fast-forwarding your kitchen's efficiency into the future while embracing the warm design details pioneered by early furnituremakers.

LESSONS FROM THE PAST

The inspiration behind the cabinetry chosen for this redo—which is truly at the heart of the functionality of this kitchen—is Shaker and Craftsman-style furniture. The cabinetry here captures the essence of those simple yet elegant styles by echoing

Though the end of the island appears to hold apothecary drawers *below,* this is actually a door panel that opens like a dishwasher door. Inside the cabinet a shelf slides out to reveal a telephone and a writing surface in one compact location.

BEFORE

It isn't easy working in a kitchen that's beginning to disintegrate. Before remodeling the kitchen cabinets *left* were falling apart and the pink tiles were popping off the countertops.

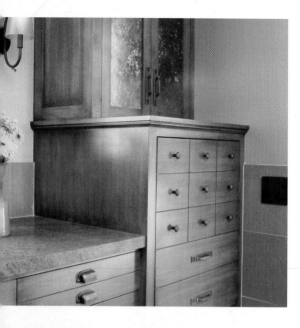

Including a few upper cabinet doors with glass panels in your kitchen provides visual variety. Translucent mica panels *left* offer a notable detail on the tall corner cabinet, which harbors a secret.

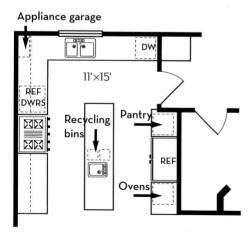

The apothecary-style drawers are actually a solid door panel that opens to reveal a dishwasher *above*, with controls neatly hidden along the top inner edge of the dishwasher door itself. Elevate your dishwasher on top of a bank of drawers like this to eliminate the need to bend when loading and unloading the appliance.

the look of old freestanding furnishings such as serving sideboards and jelly cupboards. The perimeter cabinets, for example, are fashioned from honey-hued wood and embellished modestly with clean-lined molding on door panels (drawers are sans molding), hammered-metal cup pulls, and plain wood knobs—all features you might find on an antique.

The cabinets borrow on another age-old idea: Make your kitchen an organizational success by providing an abundance of drawers. Drawers make a kitchen more convenient to work in because they offer a means for separating kitchen gear into sensible categories. Drawers also include the added bonus of presenting items in the light so you can see what you need and access it in a snap—a true back-saver for anyone who has ever bent low to rummage through the contents of a dark cabinet. Incorporate a variety of drawer depths in your plans, as this kitchen does, to handle objects ranging in bulk from stew pots and roasting pans to slim knives and flatware.

NOW YOU SEE IT

At first glance this kitchen also seems to offer a few dozen small apothecary-style drawers. In reality single doors are grooved and outfitted with multiple knobs to look like banks of small drawers. The doors open to reveal everything from a dishwasher and an appliance garage to a handy telephone and message center. Incorporate this idea in your kitchen when you want to play up an antique theme by hiding clutter or modern amenities.

Another way you can emphasize the illusion of freestanding furniture in your kitchen is to visually set the island apart

THE **PLAN**

Appliance garage

DW

11'×15'

REF
DWRS

Recycling
bins

Pantry

REF

Ovens

Even without a window you can provide a "view" above a cooktop or sink facing a solid wall. Variegated slate on the diagonal and a handsome frame of tumbled marble provide beauty above this cooktop. If you've ever spent hours scrubbing old-style burners clean, you'll appreciate the easy maintenance of a smooth glass cooktop like this one. Moldings on the exhaust hood above the cooktop are a subtle nod to Craftsman-style detailing.

BELLS AND WHISTLES

WHEN DESIGNERS Mary Fisher Knott of Mary Fisher Design and Judy Svendsen of Raven Interiors earned the opportunity to redo this kitchen for an episode of *Designers' Challenge*, the women didn't haggle for a moment about who would handle what. Between the two of them, they have 65 years of interior design experience: Mary does the function and space planning, and Judy is the shopping expert. With all that going for them, it's no wonder the designing duo has a knack for fitting loads of amenities into every kitchen—features they refer to as "bells and whistles." Smart styling ensures that the space doesn't feel overloaded, with many of the best bonuses hidden from view. Here are just a few of the perks:

AN ELEVATED DISHWASHER hides behind a cabinet door panel designed to look like a bank of apothecary drawers.

A 42-INCH-WIDE BUILT-IN REFRIGERATOR conserves space in the aisle.

THE CLEANUP SINK features dual spouts: One extra-tall gooseneck can fill the tallest vase or stock pot. Instant hot water is also available.

A MULTIFACETED PREP SINK located in the island comes with a stainless-steel bowl and a stainless-steel colander *above*—each of which fits into grooves located around the perimeter of the sink. The sink also has a board that nestles against the curve of the bowls and offers a cutting surface on one side and a work surface on the other side.

THE ISLAND has one end that harbors a hidden cabinet for the telephone on a pullout writing surface.

TWO SHALLOW DRAWERS in the kitchen pull out to reveal cutting boards for multiple cooks. Directly below the boards are drawers equipped with slots for storing knives neatly and safely.

ADDITIONAL DRAWERS below the cooktop corral cooking tools and paraphernalia. Narrow roll-out storage flanking the cooktop drawers stashes spices and other ingredients.

REFRIGERATED DRAWERS are conveniently located beside the cooktop and the prep sink in the island.

ANOTHER PULLOUT DRAWER keeps trash and recycling bins handy but out of sight.

A FLOOR-TO-CEILING CABINET beside the refrigerator is actually a roll-out pantry.

AN APPLIANCE GARAGE hides small appliances near the cleanup sink.

from surrounding cabinets by painting the base a different color, using a different countertop material, and designing the piece with feet or legs. In this kitchen the center island (shown on page 63) stands on shapely carved legs and is dressed richly in black. The honey-color limestone countertop on the island provides a dynamic contrast with the dark cabinetry below and further sets the island apart from the surrounding cabinetry, which is topped with green honed-granite countertops.

The extra-long island ensures an ample work surface for multiple cooks and features a small sink for washing vegetables or filling big pots with water. The cooktop is just a few steps away from the sink.

On the opposite side of the island, a long wall houses the built-in refrigerator, dual convection wall ovens, and a tall roll-out pantry (see the floor plan on page 64). The refrigerator (shown behind the island on page 63) is so fully integrated with matching cabinet door fronts that it virtually disappears. Hidden controls on the wall ovens keep the look of these modern appliances as unadorned as the cabinets themselves.

These finely crafted details come together to form a look that is decades away from the old pink tile and far advanced in function. To make your kitchen even more functional, design your layout around work centers. Turn the page to learn more.

Paired with the dishwasher, a larger kitchen sink provides an efficient cleanup center. (See pages 68-69 for more information on designing efficient work centers.) Plan for open shelves such as these *above* so you have a place for cookbooks, and make good use of countertop corners by penciling an appliance garage into your plans. This one hides behind the faux stack of apothecary drawers.

HONED VS. POLISHED

HOW DO YOU DECIDE between a honed-stone countertop and polished stone? (The kitchen shown on pages 62–67 features honed materials.) Polishing brings out the color and depth of the material and is a popular treatment for hard granite and marble. No-sheen honed finishes, typical for slate and limestone, can also be used for granite and marble and are gaining popularity in kitchens that showcase natural materials.

POLISHED
- Reflects light with its shiny, smooth surface.
- Suggests a "perfect" surface that looks brand-new.
- Brings out the color of the stone.
- Plays a starring role in your kitchen.

HONED
- Offers a soft, matte texture.
- Can look slightly distressed to suggest age.
- Provides less intense color.
- Lets other kitchen elements shine brightly.

Polished

Honed

CENTERS FOR EFFICIENCY

Start with a basic knowledge of the work triangle, then merge it with a smart strategy that organizes the kitchen around common activity centers, and you're on your way to an ultraefficient kitchen.

COOKING CENTER The main ingredients for your cooking center are the cooktop or range and possibly a microwave oven. A conventional oven separate from the cooktop may be a lesser-used appliance and can be located outside the work triangle. The cooking center requires storage for pots and pans, utensils, seasonings, and foods that go directly from storage container to simmering pot. The cooking surface is most efficient and safest when you include at least 18 inches of countertop on each side. This cooking center *below* is made more efficient with the addition of a chrome bar that stores utensils within easy reach of the range.

SPECIALTY CENTER Plan additional centers around specialized activities, such as baking or making coffee. A baking center might include bins for flour and sugar and a swing-up shelf for a mixer. The coffee bar *right* has a rolltop door to conceal an area for the microwave oven and for brewing coffee or tea.

PREPARATION CENTER Equip this area for preparing meals and storing dry goods. Position the refrigerator nearby and include a microwave oven, ample work surface, and a second sink. In the prep center *left* the tiered island houses a vegetable sink, a pullout cutting board, and a trash bin.

PLANNING CENTER Include space in your kitchen for answering the telephone, paying bills, and working on a computer. This oak-top desk *below* handles noncooking tasks in style. Generally, because the planning desk isn't part of cooking or cleanup, you should locate it outside the work core. To prevent this center from becoming cluttered, include storage for books, files, and electronics.

THE WORK TRIANGLE

IN THE 1950s designers developed a concept known as the work triangle to efficiently plan the layout of a kitchen. In its purest form the work triangle is the path between the refrigerator, sink, and cooktop. The goal in your kitchen is to keep the path uninterrupted by traffic or cabinetry and to minimize steps between these components.

REFRIGERATOR

COOKTOP

SINK

TODAY the work triangle remains a good gauge of your kitchen's efficiency, but modern times call for tweaking the triangle to fit your individual needs. For example you may want to position the refrigerator slightly outside the work core or on the edge of the work core, so other family members or guests can access its contents without getting in the way of the cook. Also the path through your kitchen is more likely to connect four, or even five or more, activity areas. For this reason imagine a secondary triangle overlaying the first and use it to plan steps between additional components or activity areas. For example a secondary triangle may go from a bar sink to a microwave oven to the refrigerator to accommodate fast meals and snacks.

EXPANDING ON THIS IDEA FURTHER, think about the various activities that commonly occur in your kitchen and you've grasped the additional concept of planning your kitchen around "centers." Position these centers at the logical points of the primary and secondary work triangles to create a space that functions efficiently for your lifestyle.

CLEANUP CENTER The sink will be the star of your cleanup center but it also plays a supporting role in the preparation and cooking centers (unless you include a second prep sink in your plans). If the cleanup sink is the only sink, locate it between the range and refrigerator. Other major components are the garbage disposal and the dishwasher, so dirty plates can be scraped and loaded without lost steps. If you include a trash compactor here, have it installed on the side of the sink opposite the dishwasher as shown *left*. Also include storage for dish towels, cleaning products, and a trash receptacle.

Prior to its *Designers'*
Challenge renovation,
this kitchen lacked
the storage required
by the serious cook.
Now new cabinets
and a more efficient
layout double the
storage capacity of
the room.

A COOK'S
KITCHEN

If you're serious about cooking, you'll need the proper
space, appliances, and surfaces to practice your art.

ASK ANY GOOD COOK or professional chef what he or she wants most from a kitchen, and you'll likely hear requirements for an efficient layout, quality appliances, and hardworking surfaces. Designer Maloos Anvarian, the chosen designer from an episode of *Designers' Challenge,* reworked this kitchen into a cook's dream. Here's how you can do the same in your kitchen.

ROOM TO COOK

When laying out the work core, pay close attention to appliance locations and counter space. You'll want to be able to move from one appliance to another as efficiently as possible. (For information on work triangle and workstation design, see pages 68–69.) Include a large pantry for storing ingredients and, if you specialize in a particular form of cooking such as baking, add a dedicated baking center.

BEFORE

An 8-foot-long island *opposite* serves as the primary food preparation area and is long enough to accommodate four diners. A sealed edge treatment makes the 1¼-inch-thick granite slab look more than twice as thick and gives the island more visual weight. The wall of storage *above* keeps nonperishables, baking gear, and small appliances handy yet out of sight—a vast improvement over this kitchen's previous incarnation *left*.

At the owners' requests, designer Maloos Anvarian turned the original seldom-used breakfast area into a sitting area *left*. The serving bar and art wall make it a favorite gathering spot for the owners.

A swirl-pattern metal backsplash complements the fluid pattern of the granite used behind the new professional-style range *below left*. The two-oven range was a requirement of the owners, one of whom is a serious cook.

Because there was only enough room in the kitchen for one sink, the owners opted for this two-bowl model *below right*; one bowl is large enough to hold the owners' biggest pots and pans. The artfully edged slab of vertical black monolith granite is both a conversation piece and a screen that keeps dirty dishes out of view of the sitting area.

Plan a minimum of 12 linear feet—16 linear feet is better—of cabinetry and countertops to accommodate food preparation and storage. This kitchen has nearly 25 linear feet of countertops and 30 linear feet of cabinetry storage. Countertop placement should also include a minimum of 15 inches of landing space near all the appliances (refrigerator, range, dishwasher, and microwave). These landings can be shared. Allow at least 3 feet for walkways and 4 feet if it's a traffic aisle in a work area or if two or more cooks will be crossing paths. Make sure that entry doors, cabinet doors, and appliance doors open without interference and don't obstruct walkways. (For information on accessible design, see pages 56–61.)

APPLIANCE PERFORMANCE

For better cooking performance splurge on a dual-fuel range. According to a recent survey most gourmet cooks prefer gas for surface cooking and electricity for baking. For more cooking power select a professional-style range like the one chosen for this kitchen. Most residential ranges typically offer burner capacities with adjustment ranges from 1,000 Btus to 10,000 Btus. Professional-style ranges span from 500 Btus (for delicate sauces and melting chocolate) to 15,000 Btus (for instant searing of meat). Stainless-steel enclosures and cast-iron burner grates can also withstand decades of daily wear and tear.

Today's refrigerators offer temperature zones for optimal food storage. Bottom-freezer models, fitted with drawer-style freezer sections, have made a comeback due to their ease of use. Professional-style built-in refrigerators with separate freezers, as the owners selected for this kitchen, provide the greatest capacity. If you need more storage flexibility, add a refrigerator drawer, as shown on page 25.

When it comes to dishwashers, two is the chef's mantra. If you don't want to give up storage for a second unit, the decision these owners made, add a smaller dish drawer, as shown on page 41. (For information on appliance costs see pages 179–181.)

THE **PLAN**

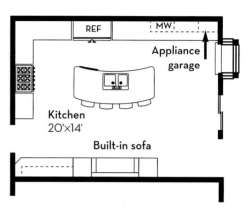

REF   MW

Appliance garage

Kitchen
20'x14'

Built-in sofa

TOP COUNTERS

Chefs often choose a granite surface when outfitting their own kitchens. In commercial kitchens the choice is typically stainless steel. The reason? Granite is available in a range of colors and patterns, is impervious to heat and scratches, and its cool, smooth surface is excellent for rolling out pastries. Stainless steel is sanitary and affordably priced. For more flexibility mix countertop materials to match the kinds of food you prepare: For instance use granite for rolling out dough and butcher block for chopping veggies and cutting bread.

In this kitchen the owners brought in more color and pattern by choosing two different granites; a fluid-pattern granite tops the island and stove backsplash, while a solid black granite covers the perimeter counters. (For more information on surfaces, see pages 28–29. For information on kitchen lighting, turn the page.)

Instead of tossing out an extra piece of granite, the designer used it as an attractive screen that keeps the sink out of view of the seating area.

THE RIGHT LIGHT

As shown in the kitchen on pages 70–73 and highlighted here, proper lighting accentuates the best aspects of a kitchen and makes cooking chores easier on the eyes.

ACCENT LIGHTING Accent lighting draws attention to focal-point features. To be effective it needs to be three to five times brighter than the ambient light in the room. Accent lighting is often found inside a display cabinet *above*, illuminating an art wall, or installed on top of upper cabinets. Upper cabinet lights or rope lights installed in the toe-kick area are examples of accent lights that also make excellent night-lights.

AMBIENT LIGHTING Ambient, or general, lighting illuminates an entire room. It often comes from ceiling-mounted fixtures or, in the case of this kitchen, from a multitude of cable lights *below* that encompasses the work core. During the day the large skylight in this kitchen also provides ambient light.

LIGHT OUTPUT

THE LIGHT output (lumens) of the bulb used in your fixture determines how much light the fixture gives out. If you experience glare, the light output may be too high. If headaches or eyestrain occur, the light may be too dim. To save energy costs choose bulbs with the light output you need and the lowest wattage. To reduce the possibility of an electrical fire, never exceed the wattage maximum supplied by the light fixture manufacturer. Color selections also affect illumination. A wall painted with flat white paint reflects 70 percent of the light that hits it. A black granite countertop or floor reflects only 10 percent of the light that hits it.

TASK LIGHTING Task lighting brightens various work surfaces. Undercabinet lights brighten the work surface near the appliance garage, as shown on page 71, and pendant lights illuminate the island work surface, as shown on page 70. Halogen table lamps *left* offer an excellent source of reading light near the love seat.

A **KITCHEN** FOR EVERY **STYLE**

Be it a galley or a great room, today's kitchen is the hub for family gatherings, entertaining, cooking, and dining. Because it is the favorite place to congregate in the home, it's important to decorate the room to reflect your personality and suit the way you live. Peruse these pages to see kitchens decorated in warm French country and classic Mediterranean styles as well as many others. Learn how to instill the elements of a favorite scheme into your own kitchen and the connecting rooms using color, accessories, decorative moldings, furnishings, and more.

TIMELESS CONTEMPORARY

Welcoming contemporary style, as this kitchen proves, is sure to withstand the test of time.

AFTER A BUSY DAY, no one wants to bring tension home and live with it. This contemporary kitchen uses warm wood tones, enticing architecture, colorful accessories, and an inviting demeanor to melt away stress and allow the owners to leave their cares at the door. You can get the same calming, clean-lined character in your kitchen by adopting the style strategies used in this kitchen.

FURNISHED ELEGANCE

Anyone can plan a kitchen open to the family room, but it takes thoughtful features to avoid the most common design clashes: a style that's too utilitarian and preparation messes in sight. These can visually disrupt adjoining living areas and stir up stress.

You can seamlessly meld the kitchen with connecting spaces by making the work core as hospitable as any living room or family room. Success begins with cabinetry reminiscent of fine furniture.

Gentle curves on the island and lighting above provide eye-pleasing visual elements that introduce the kitchen *opposite* to the rest of the family room, which is out of camera view on the right. Stainless-steel appliances provide a timeless quality that complements the natural cherry wood cabinetry.

CONTEMPORARY ELEGANCE

WHEN DESIGNING your contemporary kitchen, remember these guidelines:

CLEAN LINES. Contemporary style is straightforward. Fussy, intricate designs, such as highly carved wood, don't fit.

CURVES. Soften an abundance of hard edges by tossing in a few curves, such as a rounded countertop, a curving wall, or softly shaped light fixtures.

WOODS. Cabinetry and other furnishings made of wood help make a contemporary kitchen warm and welcoming. Select wood with uncomplicated grain patterns, such as maple.

FABRIC. Contemporary kitchens welcome fabric, but stick with solids or patterns that are simple or widely spaced.

ACCESSORIES. Inject the space with colors you love using a variety of contemporary, clean-lined accessories, such as oversize platters and sculptural vases.

For more information on **contemporary style**, visit *HGTV.com/designstyles*

A ledge on the island end intercepts the glass tabletop, which also rests on a custom-made base. The tactic achieves a seamless transition from island to table.

DEFINITIVE CHARACTER

WHEN YOUR HOME LACKS walls between the kitchen and surrounding spaces, you can depend on some style-conscious devices to define areas:

COLOR. Vary colors or shades to define one area from the next. Architect and builder Phillip Vlieger, who designed this kitchen, uses wall color to identify autonomous architectural features. "The wall colors are very carefully selected," he says. "Choosing unique shades for specific walls enhances the architecture." Between the kitchen and formal dining room, a floating wall—designed with a pass-through (see page 78)—sports a color that isn't used anywhere else in the house.

FLOORING. Changing flooring materials, such as transitioning from a wood floor in the kitchen to carpeting in the family room, adds interest and helps differentiate one space from another. Inlays can customize the look of a wood floor and allow you to visually draw a border, for example, around the kitchen work core.

FURNISHINGS. Designers have long said that furniture looks best pulled away from the wall. Pulling a sofa and sofa table perpendicular across an adjoining family room is also a good way to define the seating area from the breakfast area and make the conversation grouping feel cozier.

FABRIC. Hang sheers or other fabric between spaces to add softness and color while defining activity areas and providing privacy when desired.

ARCHITECTURE. Changing floor levels or ceiling heights easily defines one area from the next while creating visual interest.

To communicate furniturelike qualities via a center island, shy away from standard hard-lined rectangles and needlessly fussy doors and drawers or intricate hardware. The family room side of this island, for example, poses a soft curve, stainless-steel "legs," clean-lined molding, and a niche for display (see *opposite* and page 78). Quality select cherry wood construction also makes this kitchen centerpiece more akin to a good piece of furniture, rather than a convergence of standard cabinet boxes.

Repeat similar furniturelike characteristics when you select perimeter cabinetry. Here European-style frameless construction with hidden hardware communicates an unfettered custom quality that's enhanced by select cherry wood. Whenever possible include display features in your perimeter cabinetry—just as you would show off treasures in a living room. These perimeter cabinets feature a series of lighted boxes (see page 82 *below*) that draw the eye up to the ceiling level.

ON THE LEVEL

Just as cabinetry can lure your gaze, it's also an effective view-blocking tool. This multilevel island *opposite* features the highest countertop on the family room side of the space to conceal messes at the island sink and beyond. Portions of the cherry wood ledge widen to double as a dining room sideboard and can easily serve a buffet-style meal. The ledge drops down several inches to a large preparation area that's surfaced with granite and equipped with a stainless-steel sink. (Granite repeats on the perimeter cabinetry for an abundant durable work surface.) A glass-top dining table (see page 79) adjoins the side of the island outside the work core, providing another integrated level.

Furniturelike qualities, such as the legs and molding on the island, make this kitchen feel more like a living space. Eliminating visible hardware on the perimeter cabinets keeps the look serene.

81

Granite countertops bring additional elegance to the kitchen. Mounting the stainless-steel sink beneath the material repeats the streamlined look established by the cabinetry.

Though the family room is completely open to the kitchen, this floating wall *above* divides the kitchen from the formal dining room. This pass-through makes serving and cleanup easier.

Continuing the granite on the backsplash *right* keeps the look uninterrupted. A few select accessories add visual appeal and help maintain the clutter-free zone.

Though these varying levels are functional, they bring their own brand of architectural beauty to the kitchen.

While the multiple levels of an island give interest, your appliances should take a less prominent role in a contemporary kitchen that's open to the family room. Select good-quality models that operate silently and fit smoothly with the surrounding cabinetry.

FIXTURE FLOURISH

Though this kitchen takes the job of performing as a stress-free hub of the house seriously, remember that there is always room for a fun finishing flourish. On page 78, for example, notice how the lighting track sweeps across the ceiling, following the curve of the island below. Pendants dressed in spring green-color shades provide task lighting for the work surfaces, while an unexpected bold red-shaded fixture sheds light on the table.

To discover more ways to make your contemporary kitchen inviting and warm, turn the page.

Even in a clean, contemporary kitchen, there's room for treasures. These lighted upper cabinets *above* put special pieces on display; the cabinets also provide pleasing mood lighting during evenings.

INVITING CONTEMPORARY

The best contemporary kitchens are as warm and welcoming as they are clean-lined. Consider incorporating these features from the kitchen shown on pages 78–83 to make yours a classic.

FLOOR SHOW Continue the warmth established by your cabinet wood choice to the floor level. This floor *above* is primarily select cherry wood like the cabinetry. Wide inlaid bands of red birch add interest and align with columns between the kitchen and adjoining family room. You can also warm a contemporary kitchen floor with an area rug that features a simple design.

NATURAL TENDENCIES You needn't depend on dark stains to make a contemporary kitchen warm—this light wood *below* increases the hospitality factor of the room and doesn't date the look as dark wood can. Architect Phillip Vlieger rarely uses stains on the woods in the homes he builds. "Natural wood never goes out of style," he says.

GOOD HUES Make a contemporary kitchen more fun and playful by adding accessories in assertive colors. These vases *below* introduce stimulating sculptural shapes and eye-pleasing color.

FASHIONABLE FIXTURES Proper lighting helps make a kitchen more inviting. (For tips on lighting your kitchen, turn to page 74.) This track lighting fixture *above* adds warming color and style over the island.

SOFT SENSATIONS Find ways to bring fabric into your contemporary kitchen to soften hard edges, but avoid frills. This two-tone shimmery fabric *left* highlights the eating area of the kitchen by adding subtle shine and color to the chair seats.

Pretty blue-and-white ceramic canisters keep flours and sugars handy for baking. Other less-aesthetically pleasing baking supplies, including a stand mixer, hide inside the appliance garage shown on page 92.

ARTFUL ACCESSORIZING

Just as a blank canvas inspires an artist to create, let a kitchen dressed in white serve as a clean slate for artful accessorizing.

Although the display cabinets in this kitchen *right* appear to have no backs, it is just an illusion. The cabinet back panels are actually tiled, a solution that ensures the sturdiness of the cabinets is not compromised by removing the backs. The deep blue tiles provide interesting contrast against the white edges of the plates and frame of the tile mural.

WHEN WHITE IS USED as a background color, its light-reflecting qualities make it a decorator's dream—it can be invigorated with warm hues or soothed with cool tones. Neutral tones, such as creams, soft beiges, natural wood tones, grays, and blacks, can also be introduced to bring in even more visual interest. In these two kitchens with white cabinets, deep blue accents—a tiled backsplash on the kitchen *above right* and decorative accessories in the kitchen *below right*—contrast with the cabinets to create a sophisticated, soothing ambience. On pages 88–89 warm color accents create a cozier environment.

PERSONAL TOUCHES

One of the easiest ways to personalize an all-white kitchen is to display the items you love. If you have a prized collection of colorful

As these two kitchens *above* show, accessories bring a white kitchen to life. In the kitchen *top* a collection of blue transferware plates served as inspiration for the colorful tile backsplash. Although the permanent features in the kitchen *above* are more neutral (the granite counter is gray, and the backsplash is glass block), the blue accessories still stand out against the white cabinets.

Bright yellow flowers, pottery, and wooden baskets warm up a display niche in this white kitchen *above*. An arched fascia and undercabinet lights accent a trio of framed prints.

pottery, china, or stemware, display it behind glass doors or in open plate racks. If the pattern on your china is a favorite feature, look for a plate rack where plates rest flat against the wall (see page 93) instead of perpendicular to the wall.

If you have more than one set of china or stoneware, show off each set seasonally for an instant accessory update. If you don't have a second set of dishes or if the ones you have aren't display-worthy, look for bargains online, in catalogs, or in secondhand stores to introduce fresh color and patterns inexpensively for holidays or whenever the mood strikes.

For an added jolt of color, install colorful knobs and handles that complement your displays. (For more information on installing cabinetry hardware, see page 121.)

Transform plain backsplashes into display places for framed art as shown *left* or add a tile mural, as shown on page 87, that is both artistic and functional. To combine more form with function, invest in beautiful ceramic canisters and decorative platters and bowls *left* that you can use to showcase baked goods or garden fare.

A neutral-color tile backsplash *above right* serves as an attractive background for any combination of colorful accessories. Just change the countertop display to alter the look of the kitchen.

Red earthenware plates *right* fill the open plate rack and bring vibrant color and welcome pattern into the all-white room.

To make your displays even more personal and colorful, exhibit items that reveal something about your family, perhaps where you have traveled or lived. The wine caddy *opposite* holds wines purchased on a recent vineyard tour.

To keep countertops from becoming cluttered, stash small appliances behind closed doors or in appliance garages. Then dot the open surface with more attractive fare that adds splashes of bold color, such as pottery, fruit baskets, and fresh flowers or green plants. For advice on how to arrange items, see "The Art of Display" *opposite*. To personalize basic all-white kitchen cabinetry with custom-look features, turn the page.

An artful display of fresh-from-the garden flowers and fruits *above left* invites guests to come in and enjoy the hospitality.

These small drawers *left* hold car keys, writing utensils, and pads of sticky notes, keeping the clutter off the countertops. The shiny black knobs and painted rope molding pop against the white cabinets.

A wine caddy *above* gives the countertop a custom touch.

Glass blocks with a diamond pattern sparkle in the sunlight and twinkle at night when the streetlights are on. The glass-block windows *above right* replace a more traditional backsplash, allowing in sunlight without giving up the storage space consumed by a traditional window.

THE ART OF DISPLAY

THINK OF EACH glass-fronted cabinet or open shelf as a seesaw: Arrange accessories to create a comfortable balance.

USE COLOR TO UNIFY YOUR DISPLAY. On page 87, top photo, blue plates and a blue tile backsplash add a touch of color to a mostly white kitchen. The kitchen on page 88 uses creamy neutrals to complement the warm wood tones of the floor and the antique table.

REMEMBER: BIGGER IS ALMOST ALWAYS BETTER. In addition to the necessary stacks of plates and bowls, add larger pottery pieces or a framed print to visually balance the utilitarian items.

THERE'S SOMETHING ATTRACTIVE ABOUT UNEVEN NUMBERS. In decorating three is the magic number. Three canisters, three bottles of oil, three green plants, and even three mismatched items meld together to create a natural balance. If you need to add more items to fill a larger expanse of space, increase the amount by two—to five, seven, or nine items—to create an eye-pleasing display.

TAKE TIME TO ARRANGE PIECES in several different ways, and then choose the one that's the most attractive to your eye.

CUSTOM TOUCHES

Readily available stock options, such as these, customize the white stock cabinets shown on pages 87–91. Some options open the door to adding eye-pleasing, easy-change accent color.

CLEAR THE CLUTTER Ready-made appliance garages, like the one *below*, fit between the countertop and wall cabinet, keeping small appliances and other kitchen tools handy yet out of sight. The units come in several sizes, paint finishes (or unfinished so you can add your personal touch), and styles to fit corner or straight-on configurations.

CUSTOM-LOOK DETAILS Acrylic plastic display bins *above* are available as stock or semicustom options in many cabinetry lines. Perk up white cabinets by filling the bins with colorful candies or just-for-fun items, such as buttons or marbles. Mix and match stock and semicustom features made by the same manufacturer so colors and details will match.

STORE IN STYLE A ready-made plate rack like the one *above* can be purchased at any home center. Use it to store everyday plates in hues you love. Paint or stain the rack to contrast with or complement your cabinets. Hang the rack near the sink or dishwasher.

SPECIAL DETAILS Rope molding purchased from a home center adorns the top and bottom of the once-plain cabinets *left*. To paint unfinished molding, spray it with a quality primer; let dry. Brush or spray on two coats of a paint color that complements your cabinets; allow the paint to dry between coats.

HORIZONTAL PLATE RACK

IF A READY-MADE plate rack won't work in your kitchen configuration, add a plate rail to a breakfast room wall. Although ready-made versions are widely available, you can also make your own from salvaged door headers or home center materials. These 36-inch-long rails are made from 1×6 clear pine toppers and 1×3 boards that have been routed for plates. Fasten the pieces together with wood screws, trim them with decorative molding, and then prime and paint your creation.

93

Soft green painted walls provide a cheerful foil for the white cabinetry and new black solid surface countertops.

HIDE AND SEEK

Use clever cottage-style elements to conceal some kitchen features while beautifully revealing others.

Even the cabinet shelves earn a fresh start with toile-pattern shelf liner *right* that's partially visible through the frosted-glass doors.

CABINET DOORS with glass fronts add interest to a kitchen by showing off dishware and collections. But it's also possible to overdo a good thing, as was the case in this kitchen *below,* where a multitude of glass doors—though charming—overpowered the space. The abundance of panes created another problem: The chore of keeping cabinet interiors constantly neat or tolerating disorderly contents always on view.

The multipane doors, typical of cottage styling, posed an immediate virtue for the kitchen, which was otherwise awash in too much white. If you face similar kitchen style issues at your house, borrow these clever fixes.

HIDDEN TALENT
To obscure the contents of glass door cabinetry without ruining the enchanting style of the doors, use glass-etching cream or frosted-glass spray paint (both are available at crafts stores) to frost the interior side of the glass. The resulting translucent effect allows the colors and shapes of the cabinet contents to show without revealing too much detail. To

distinguish some of the doors from others, use a stencil and etching cream or frosted-glass spray paint to apply a diamond-pattern vine detail instead of frosting the glass. (Garden elements play up a cottage style kitchen. To learn more about the elements of cottage style, see "Cottage-Style Starters" on page 96.)

Finish the cabinet interiors with shelf liner that wipes clean. For these cabinets the shelf liner in a black and white toile pattern *above right* enhances the cottage character of the space and is partially visible through the newly etched panes.

CLASSIC COTTAGE ADDITIONS
Give a kitchen more cottage character by adding furniture details and other elements that will make the cabinets look like vintage freestanding pieces—something you might

A section of cabinetry between the range and refrigerator gains decorative brackets and bun feet to mimic the look of a freestanding hutch *above.* New subway tiles dress the backsplash. The tiles are installed on the vertical as a nod to the lines of the cabinetry.

BEFORE

Before the makeover this kitchen *right* was awash in white, and the glass doors put too much on display.

COTTAGE-STYLE STARTERS

INTRODUCE THESE CHARACTERISTICS in your kitchen to capture the charm of cottage style:

DOOR DYNAMICS. If your kitchen features plain cabinet doors, add beaded-board panels or multipane glass doors (just a few will do). You can also finish exposed cabinet sides or the backsplash with beaded board framed with molding.

COLOR. Soft white, ivory, cream, and pastel colors can enhance a cottage-style kitchen. Introduce these colors using paint, fabric, accessories, or tile.

GARDEN GRACES. Cottage style is inherently connected to casual gardens. Bring in fresh flowers and incorporate elements reminiscent of the garden, such as the small planters on page 94 and the flower-filled vase on page 95.

FABRIC. Depend on traditional fabrics to complement your cottage setting, such as toile, ticking, or garden motifs (the banding shown on the valance shown at the top left of page 99 is a great example).

ACCESSORIES. Shop flea markets and antiques stores for vintage pieces—anything from old clocks to dishware—to decorate your kitchen.

Brackets nailed beneath the upper cabinets *left* lend another decorative furniture-quality feature to the kitchen.

This message center *above* brings inviting, casual cottage style to the backdoor hallway. To make your own, purchase a frame and fit cork squares inside the frame. If desired cover the cork with fabric; wrap the fabric to the back of the cork squares and secure it with hot glue or staples.

To further differentiate the look of the "hutch" section of cabinetry, these glass doors *right* are treated to a stenciled vine design that's created with frosted-glass spray paint on the interior side of the glass.

find at Grandma's house. For example purchase short turned legs or bun feet, paint or stain them to match cabinetry, and tuck them into the toe-kick space. You can also add decorative brackets beneath upper cabinets to create the look of a freestanding hutch (see page 95 *bottom right*). In this instance the bun feet gain a notable detail with the addition of a thin block of wood painted white and slipped beneath each foot.

If cabinet doors or drawers lack interest, add molding to the fronts or edges. *Below right* 1½-inch-wide flat trim adorns the fronts of the lower doors.

To further develop the classic cottage look, black solid-surfacing countertops

replace white ceramic tile. (Black and white is considered a classic combination in any style.) Backsplashes gain a refreshing vintage spin with subway tiles installed vertically. Spring green-color paint brightens walls and makes the white cabinetry and black countertops visually pop. The refreshing green color continues into the adjoining back entry, where the addition of a message center and shelf offers a place for keys, coats, and notes. Accessories lend finishing touches of cottage charm throughout, such as ceramic containers of plants and flowers and a black and white valance with a cottage garden border (see page 94). For additional window treatment ideas, turn the page.

(see page 95 *bottom right*)
(see page 94)

GLASS ALTERNATIVES

FROSTING THE GLASS in upper cabinet doors is just one option for concealing what's inside. Also consider these alternative ideas:

STAINED-GLASS PAINTS. These colored paints, in liquid and spray form, are formulated for glass and create the illusion of stained glass.

TRANSPARENT OR TRANSLUCENT PAPERS. Look for beautiful papers at an art store. Use spray adhesive to secure the paper to the back side of the glass.

ACRYLIC PANELS. Remove glass panels and replace them with colored or textured acrylic panels.

TEXTURED GLASS. Substitute clear glass with textured glass.

FABRIC. You can remove glass panels or leave them in and add fabric to conceal cabinet interiors. Use hook-and-loop tape to secure fabric to the insides of the cabinet doors or gather and staple the fabric in place. You can also thread rod-pocket panels onto small dowels installed on the backs of the doors.

A bun foot—primed and painted white—is inserted into the toe-kick space *far left* to add a detail reminiscent of a hutch. A wood base, cut and painted to match the foot, was slipped underneath for more visual impact.

Cabinet doors *left* gained a more substantial look with the addition of 1½-inch-wide flat trim secured to the front, creating the look of a recessed panel.

WOW WINDOWS

Dress up your kitchen and dining room windows with treatments such as these that usher in additional color, softness, and character.

SHAPED SOLUTION Let light and breezes flow freely into your kitchen with a treatment that uses minimal fabric. The triangular treatment *left* uses gingham fabric that would fit nicely in a cottage-style kitchen; the tassel fringe lends a touch of finery.

LOVELY LAYERS Pair window treatments with a wooden cornice board for a layered look and added dimension. This wooden cornice board *below* is topped with crown molding, making it an elegant addition to a traditional kitchen. The toile tapestry-fabric cloud shade mounted behind the cornice adds vibrant color and softens the hard lines of the cabinetry and backsplash tiles. The shade can be lowered or raised easily with the tug of a cord.

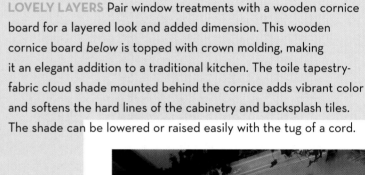

EMBELLISHED VALANCE To make a kitchen look warm and welcoming without overwhelming the room, use a valance that blends with the wall color. Old-fashioned white buttons set off this draped and pleated valance *above*, making it a good choice for a vintage-style or farmhouse kitchen. The focal point of the kitchen is the glass-fronted cabinets, not the window; the cream-color fabric matches the walls and keeps the attention on the cabinets.

VALANCE Use a valance to play up a palette. In the kitchen on pages 94–97, a white and black fabric valance *above* replaces the dated scalloped wood fascia and repeats the classic color combination of the cabinetry and countertops. The garden-motif border makes it a suitable choice for a cottage-style space.

ROMAN SHADE To avoid soiled fabric purchase or make window treatments that can pull up and out of the way when food preparation is in full swing. These translucent Roman shades *above* suit the tranquil look of the traditionally styled kitchen but are simple enough to complement a contemporary space.

CAFE CURTAINS Because windows bring the view inside, let your setting inspire the fabric selection. Views of an orchard served as the inspiration for this breakfast room window treatment *left*. Pleated fruit-print fabric valances add cheerful color; the checkerboard motif of the painted walls reappears in smaller form in the lining of the valances and on the top ties of the matching cafe curtains. The style and pattern of the curtains make them a pretty addition to a French country kitchen.

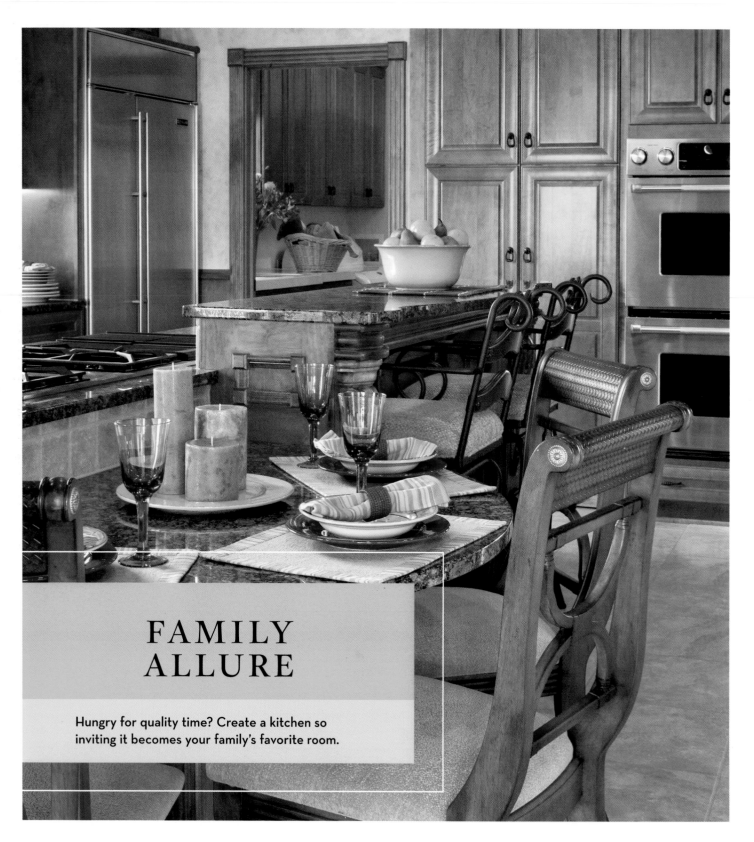

FAMILY ALLURE

Hungry for quality time? Create a kitchen so inviting it becomes your family's favorite room.

The lowest level of the island *opposite* is the right height for sit-down meals. Adding graceful scroll-back chairs—wood renditions at the table and metal stools at the island—elegantly suits the old-world theme.

LIKE A GOOD DAY FISHING, you only need to include some enticing "bait" in your kitchen plans to reel your family in for quality time together. This 11×16-foot kitchen pairs up with an 8×16-foot sitting area (see page 104) to offer a generous space for working and gathering. The unmistakable drawing card is the welcoming old-world atmosphere.

GET THE LOOK

Warm woods. Maple cabinets suit the period theme. The rich coffee-color stain wraps the room like a cozy blanket on a cold day. Most any type of wood—pine, oak, walnut, and mahogany—will work in an old-world kitchen. The main goal is to select stains in darker tones.

Earthy surfaces. Granite countertops stand up to everything your family can dish out, and the stone complements the warmhearted spirit of the wood with speckles of brown, black, and cream. Creamy hues continue to the floor, where the tiles mimic the look of well-aged travertine but are actually affordable and readily available ceramic. When you're ready to select countertops and flooring for your old-world kitchen, look for natural materials or look-alikes and remember that a worn or weathered appearance is an asset.

Architectural extras. While the high ceiling here offers a note of old-world grandeur, the diamond-patterned coffered wood beams overhead (see page 106) combine with faux-painted ceiling insets to make the room feel intimate instead of cold and cavernous. A fireplace in the sitting area promises more comfort and another place to chat in a pair of cushy club chairs. If your tastes lean toward simpler details, it's fine to incorporate clean-lined moldings and cabinetry features into your old-world kitchen. Maintain the substantial size of moldings and select more rustic finishes to play up the look.

Stainless-steel appliances, such as this pair of double ovens *above*, provide a handsome, gleaming contrast to the dark-stained maple cabinetry. The wine chiller allows the family kitchen to make an easy transition for adult get-togethers. To see the lower-level wine cellar in this same house, turn to page 32.

ELEMENTS OF OLD-WORLD STYLE

RICH, DARK WOODS

SUBSTANTIAL MOLDINGS

ARCHITECTURAL ADD-ONS, such as carved wood corbels and wood onlays.

STONE FEATURES, such as granite countertops.

WEATHERED FINISHES for flooring (wood, stone, or stone look-alikes) and backsplashes (stone or stone look-alikes).

To learn more about the elements of old-world style, turn to page 106.

For more information on **old-world style,** visit *HGTV.com/designstyles*

A wall of patio doors and a large window over the sink balance the old-world warmth of this kitchen with generous doses of sunlight. Though the space is grand, the multilevel island and other amenities make it an ideal kitchen for a family.

Old world meets modern day at the fireplace *opposite*, where the elegantly carved fireplace surround coexists peacefully with the plasma-screen television above—an ideal location for viewing from anywhere in the sitting area and kitchen.

PLEASE THE FAMILY

Here are more features that work with the old-world flavor of the kitchen yet enhance the family-friendly atmosphere:

Island oasis. Cabinetry and countertops match the rest of the kitchen, allowing the island (see pages 102–103) to blend with the setting. The family functionality, however, is anything but "old world." Three countertop levels handle multiple activities: cooking chores for the mid-level, quick snacks or conversing with the cook at the bar-height ledge, and a round table-height surface for sit-down meals. Chairs and stools ensure the island can handle a family-size gathering. If you have very young children, for safety's sake relocate the cooktop to a perimeter countertop and outfit the island top with a second sink, or reserve the surface as a solid countertop for food preparation.

Appliance pluses. A 48-inch downdraft cooktop, a built-in refrigerator, a warming drawer, a walk-in pantry (concealed behind tall cabinet doors), a dishwasher, and double ovens make this a full-service kitchen that is sure to accommodate a busy family. You may find the warming drawer (see page 103) especially handy if your children are involved in a variety of different activities: You can easily keep dinner warm for anyone coming home late from a music lesson or sports practice.

A little extra. The built-in plasma-screen television above the fireplace *opposite* means that everyone can enjoy the big game whether they're relaxing around the fireplace or participating in other activities in the work core. If you don't have a sitting area or family room adjoining your kitchen, hide a small television inside an upper cabinet or consider one of the space-saving flip-down flat screens that install beneath upper cabinets. Both options preserve an old-world atmosphere.

To learn more about creating an inviting old-world kitchen, turn the page.

ISLANDS OF OPPORTUNITY

REGARDLESS OF THE STYLE you choose for your kitchen, avoid the "deserted island" syndrome at your house by creating an island that caters to kids:

THINK SNACKS. Kids are always hungry after school. Equip your island with a microwave oven they can easily reach for heating frozen nibbles and popcorn. Provide a ledge with stools that encourage your crew to have a seat and tell you all about their day.

INVITE HOMEWORK AND PROJECTS. Create a space to spread out worksheets and books with comfortable chairs and a roomy table connected to the island. Keep in mind that a solid granite countertop lets pencils and pens press enthusiastically to paper without permanently engraving the table surface (which tends to happen with wood tables). An island table can also be a good spot for doing crafts and science projects.

STORE THEIR STUFF. Reserve one island cabinet for paper plates, plastic cups, cereal bowls, crafts supplies, and whatever kid-oriented items you want your children to easily reach. Offering one organized storage location encourages cleanups too.

MAKE CONNECTIONS. Equip the island with electric outlets and modem connections to accommodate notebook computers and other electronic devices kids use.

OLD—WORLD ELEMENTS

Enjoy the warm, stately look of old-world Europe, such
as the kitchen shown here and on pages 100–105, without
forgoing function. Start with these elegant elements.

HIGH AMBITIONS Rather than squash the grandeur of the space with a low ceiling—or worse, soffits over cabinetry, which can date the look—extend cabinetry to the ceiling and put out-of-reach storage space to work as a display case. These small upper cabinets *left* feature wrought-iron grilles over glass for a touch of old-world craftsmanship. Lighting in the cabinet interiors illuminates collections and also serves as a convenient, low-intensity night-light for late-night snackers.

The refined, handcrafted look of wood continues to the extensive use of substantial moldings throughout the room, including deep dentil crowns at the ceiling and wide casements around doors and windows. A carved wood onlay adds a flourish at the top of the patio door shown at *left*.

The ceiling *left* provides more old-world "wow" power in this kitchen. Beams form a diamond-patterned coffered ceiling, which is a series of crisscrossing beams with open ceiling spaces between wood members. The handsome, nicely detailed beams offer a note of function to the space by providing a place for recessed lighting fixtures. Moldings on the sides of the beams harbor a secret—rope lighting that can be left on when other room lights are out, producing a romantic glow and enhancing the architectural lines of the ceiling.

Rather than leave the open ceiling spaces between beams stark white, faux painting in rich coffee and cream colors makes this overhead feature one cohesive highlight.

MOLDED IMAGE Thinking of old-world Europe often conjures images of grand estates and stately castles. Bringing a touch of those romantic residences into your own kitchen is easy when you add stone. In this kitchen tumbled stone backsplashes look almost ancient but offer a surface that stands up to water and grease. More importantly the stone serves as a lovely backdrop for the wood cabinetry, moldings, and sconce lighting *above*.

DYNAMIC DETAILS Carved wood features complete your old-world kitchen and can be added to your existing cabinetry. Corbels—small or hefty, such as this one *left* that's located on one island corner—lend handcrafted character. Look for these architectural carvings in catalogs and online.

MORE OLD— WORLD IDEAS

CABINETRY If stained wood doesn't suit your tastes, opt for painted wood. Select a finish technique that looks aged, such as black-painted cabinetry with the color rubbed off around hardware and on door and drawer edges.

COUNTERTOPS While granite offers gorgeous natural color that complements old-world style, other countertop materials will work. Consider limestone for its worn appearance or wood countertops for warmth. A solid, dark-color solid-surfacing material or soapstone works well with the rich look equated with this style.

FLOORING The travertinelike tiles in this kitchen look beautiful, but if you prefer something easier on the legs, choose wood or laminate. Today's laminates come in a variety of convincing look-alikes, including wood, tile, or stone.

APPLIANCES Stainless steel works well with an old-world theme, but you can conceal appliance doors of any finish with panels that match the kitchen cabinetry.

PALETTE Colors in your old-world kitchen should be neutral or rich and regal.

Hand-painted stools and a colorful tile backsplash provide visual balance against the colorfully painted cabinets on the opposite side of the room (shown on pages 110–111.)

TRUE COLORS

Give your kitchen a one-of-a-kind look with lively colors and hand-painted designs.

MANY KITCHEN makeovers start with color, from choosing the perfect hue for the walls to finding the right color of countertop and cabinets. Before making these decisions you must choose a complementary color palette. With more than 10 million shades to choose from, it can be difficult to narrow your selection down to the handful that will look beautiful in your home. Use this kitchen and the information on pages 114–115 for tips and tricks to help you select the palette that's right for you.

INSPIRATIONS

Interior designers often start the color-planning process with an inspirational piece, such as a favorite fabric, hand-painted pottery, or a colorful throw rug. Designers pull out a primary, secondary, and accent color from the piece, creating a color palette with very little effort. Selecting colors this way eliminates worries about whether chosen colors will

match or clash. If they work together in the inspirational piece, they will work together in a room.

If you know that certain elements, such as art, antiques, or a tile mural, will be a part of your kitchen design, let them help guide your color choices. Use them to match cabinetry finishes, countertops, and paint colors. In this kitchen a mural painted on a table in an adjacent room inspired the owners to adorn the cabinets along one wall of the kitchen with similar hand-painted designs. The cheerful palette chosen for the cabinetry murals mimics those used on the table. Secondary and accent colors used throughout the room are also pulled from the original tabletop design.

The medium wood tone of the birch cabinets serves as a predominant neutral color and creates a resting spot for the eye between invigorating color jolts. Raspberry walls and accents serve as the secondary color, and accessory colors

Appropriate to this kitchen, the subjects of the murals center around foods, including fruits, vegetables, pastries, and pies *above*. The owner runs a small dessert business, which makes the paintings of the baked goods seem especially sweet.

provide the remaining accent colors. Black countertops and backsplashes also work as a restful neutral. For the fail-safe color formula used in this kitchen, see "Goof-Proof Color" on page 111.

COLOR CORRECTIONS

Color can also help accentuate the architectural strengths of a room and compensate for its weaknesses. Here's how to put color to work in your kitchen.

Undersize and oversize rooms. If you want your kitchen to feel larger or smaller, think in terms of advancing and receding colors. Bright pinks, oranges, and reds advance, making walls seem closer and the room smaller. Cool colors—greens, blues, and grays—recede, seemingly pushing walls back and increasing the perceived size of a room. Because this kitchen is not overly large, the owners opted to keep the palette of advancing colors primarily on one wall to reduce their impact in regard to the perceived size of the room.

Open plans. For floor plans without obvious transitions between rooms, create planes of color to delineate different functional spaces. Pick a palette of four to six similar colors and change hues where the walls meet. The color variations create depth and contrast without jarring the senses. In this home room transitions are obvious, so color is used as a visual connecting point rather than as a separation: Similar colors in varying doses are used in each connecting room to unite the spaces.

Ceiling sensation. Not sure what color to paint the ceiling? Consider sky blue. Nature conditions us to feel comfortable and happy when that color is above us. For more help on choosing the right color palette for your kitchen, turn to page 114.

SHADE SECRETS

BEFORE you put a brush to a wall, purchase small amounts of paint and apply the colors to poster boards. Place the painted boards along each wall in the room you plan to paint. Review the colors throughout the day to ensure you've chosen the proper shades. Cool northern sunlight looks much different in relation to color than does strong directional light, and when paint covers all the walls in a room it often appears a shade or two darker.

A mural on a tabletop in an adjacent room inspired the vibrant color scheme of this kitchen. To ensure the owners got exactly the look they wanted, they hired the same team of artists to paint this row of cabinets and the decorative knobs used throughout the room.

GOOF-PROOF COLOR

IF YOU ARE uncertain how big each dose of color should be, use a 60-30-10 formula as a foolproof guide. According to the formula, a predominant color should cover 60 percent of the room (usually the painted walls or, in the case of a kitchen, the majority of the cabinets). A secondary color covers 30 percent (window treatments, upholstery, rugs, and, in kitchens, often the walls), while accent colors account for the remaining 10 percent (artwork, pillows, hand towels, dishware, and pottery). Although you don't need to be too mathematical about these color percentages, this formula can help you decide how much of each color is adequate.

For more great ideas on **using color in your home**, visit *HGTV.com/color*

Natural surface materials, such as the slate backsplash *above,* the black granite countertop, and oak-plank floors, provide a soothing backdrop for the focal-point murals.

Because most of the artwork in the kitchen is busy and animated, the glass-front displays in the upper cabinets *opposite* stay simple. In each cabinet a Gerber daisy peeks out of a bud vase.

Although it looks like fabric, this window valance *below* is actually a wooden cornice. The fruit and flower motif ties the window dressing to the cabinet murals.

Open cubbies in the island end provide display space for plates and pottery. The same artists who painted the cabinetry murals painted the display pieces.

BAKER'S DREAM

THE FUNCTION of this kitchen is as appealing as its style. Professional-grade appliances and a step-saving L-shape layout enable the owner, a dessert caterer, to whip up her creations without wasting a moment. The granite-top center island serves as the primary food preparation center and is used for rolling out dough. A stand mixer is a permanent countertop accessory, a testament to its frequent use. For more information on functional kitchen layouts, see pages 30–31.

A range of painted knobs dots the doors of the natural wood cabinets and includes bunches of grapes and pairs of cherries *above.*

JUST YOUR SHADE

As the kitchen on pages 108–113 illustrates, color selection is personal and emotional. Choose hues for your kitchen that underscore your individuality and outlook.

BRIGHT AND LIVELY Find inspiration from an item that boasts fresh and vivid colors, as shown in the hand-painted cabinetry doors or the colorful knobs *above* and on pages 108 and 113.

KITCHEN COLOR: HOW BRAVE ARE YOU? Several different elements can bring color into the kitchen. Look *below* to find the level of commitment and impact that's right for you.

ELEMENT	COMMITMENT	IMPACT
Painted walls	**Low.** Painting walls is an inexpensive and easily changed proposition. Plus most kitchens have minimal open wall space, which prevents even the brightest of colors from overpowering a room.	**Moderate to high.** A color change can transform your room, especially when you combine it with new artwork and accessories. (For more information on the impact of accessories, see pages 86–93.)
Countertops	**High.** Countertops are one of the pricier kitchen elements to change, particularly if you plan to choose a natural stone surface. Pick a color you can live with for years to come.	**Moderate to high.** Going from light to dark or vice versa has a big impact, as does swapping a solid-color surface for a patterned surface.
Cabinets	**Moderate to high.** New cabinets are a substantial investment, but painting old ones a bold new color is low-cost and low-risk.	**High.** Whether wood tone or painted wood, colorful cabinetry alone is often enough to brighten a kitchen.
Flooring	**High.** Vinyl and laminates are less of a financial commitment, but hardwood, stone, and ceramic tiles are big-ticket items.	**Low to moderate.** Flooring is valued more for its ease of care than color impact. Its color and style may even go unnoticed.
Hardware	**Low.** It's one of the fastest and easiest elements to change—and often the most affordable.	**Low to moderate.** Knobs and pulls can add welcome splashes of color. Distinctive pieces like the knobs *left* can be surprisingly noticeable.
Appliances	**Low to high.** Special-order colors are pricey commitments, but changeable appliance panels in designer colors make for a quick and affordable update.	**High.** Anything other than white, black, or metallic stands out—and even these may serve as focal points when combined with cabinetry and wall color.

SOFT AND SUBDUED If your style is cool and understated, choose an inspiration piece that conjures similar emotions, such as a pale watercolor painting or pastel glass bottles *below*.

NATURE HIKE Are you having trouble finding something that inspires you? Cattails and meadow grasses *above* may help you visualize the perfect palette for your kitchen.

TRENDS

ACCORDING TO LEATRICE EISEMAN, the Pantone Color Institute's executive director and author of *The Color Answer Book*, this year's color palette reflects the same diversity as today's kitchen designs. She divides the palette into eight color categories:

Réalité. This color set expresses elements derived from nature. Textures and finishes often appear hand-woven or honed with subtle color undertones that add an imaginative touch to basic neutrals. Combinations include Pale Khaki, Sage, Shadow, and Gobelin Blue.

 Refresh. Imagine clean, cool morning air, crystal clear blue skies, a translucent turquoise lake, and verdant meadows. Add the tangy bite of a crisp Apple Green accent, and the refreshing view is picture perfect.

Radiance. To be radiant literally means to express joy, energy, or good health. In terms of color Radiance celebrates the glowing essence of the spectrum. Colors include Burnt Henna, Striking Purple, Purple Orchid, and Mineral Yellow.

 Relax. As the name implies, this category is expressed in mellow tones. With more presence than the lighter pastels of the past, these midtones include Pink Nectar and Banana Crepe. They are juxtaposed against colors that suggest inviting textural surfaces, such as the dark cream of Camel or the cool gray of Skyway.

RePlay. Filled with colors first cherished in the 1950s and '60s, this lively palette includes a playful mix of Jelly Bean Green and Ribbon Red or the Puccilike patterned colors of Camellia Rose and cheerful orange, lemon, and lime.

 Refinements. Also expressed as tradition with a twist, this color set keeps with the eclectic approach of mixing modern with antique. Color combinations are complex, imaginative, and artistic. Examples are grape or violet used with mossy greens and mahogany browns or Beaujolais wines and ashy blue-greens accented by a rich gold or a silvery sage.

Recurrents. This color group is reminiscent of sophisticated, urbanized film noir, where sepia overtones merge with pure white or off-white, Caviar Black, Deep Taupe, other shades of taupe, and muted grays and greens. This new take on reel-life drama offers two additional options in expressive accents of Lipstick Red or Classic Blue.

 Respite. This category includes nurturing comfort colors, such as Hay, Cinnabar, Cashew, and Southern Moss.

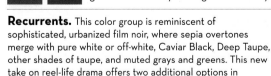

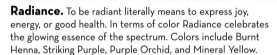

Simple additions make this once-barren kitchen feel warm and welcoming. A cool watermelon-color paint enlivens the walls, fabric window dressings soften the window casings, and new brushed-nickel handles instantly update the old painted cabinets.

FASHION FORWARD

As this $1,000 makeover proves, with the right accessories and cosmetics any kitchen can make a great first impression.

Prior to its makeover, this kitchen *right* lacked color and personality, making it feel more like a rental house than a family home.

BEFORE

PRIOR TO A MAKEOVER, this little kitchen was less than a trendsetter. White walls, white cabinets, and a jarring two-tone tile countertop *above right* made the room look sterile and uninviting—an appearance that did not match the warm and friendly personalities of the newlyweds who live there. Thanks to *Design on a Dime* team members Kristan Cunningham, Spencer Anderson, and Dave Sheinkopf, the kitchen boasts a fresh new attitude. If your kitchen needs a fashion update, make a few of these simple and affordable changes.

COLOR ADJUSTMENT

To begin your makeover choose a favorite color as your decorating mainstay, such as the pale watermelon hue used in this kitchen. Then choose one or two complementary accent colors, possibly from surfaces already in place. In this kitchen the existing tile countertop defines the accent colors,

making the lively hues appear as though they were part of the decorating scheme instead of an unwanted inheritance.

Enliven the walls with your favorite color. Then extend the hue in varying shades to a few prominent accessories, such as throw rugs and floral arrangements, to add depth and interest to the scheme. Use the other accent colors on window treatments, artwork, and additional countertop and tabletop accessories, as the *Design on a Dime* team did: A warm red hue used for the window treatments adds a splash of color against the walls, while the floorcloth and pillows sport a fresh green.

BRIGHT OUTLOOK

If your work surfaces are not adequately lit—and you don't have sufficient light for kitchen-related tasks such as cooking or cleanup—brighten the room's attitude with another light fixture or two. Many

A magnetic message board *above* fills what was once empty wall space by the refrigerator. It enables the couple to communicate as they come and go. (To make your own message board, see page 163.)

CASUAL STYLE

GIVE YOUR KITCHEN a relaxed feel with a decorating style that puts comfort first.

UNFUSSY FURNISHINGS. Carefree fabrics and unadorned furniture pieces exude casual style, the look conveyed in this modest kitchen.

MIX NOT MATCH. Choose accessories and fabrics that look good together but don't look as though they were all purchased from the same store at the same time. In this kitchen the linoleum rug complements the wall and countertop color but isn't an exact match.

SIMPLE FIXTURES. Choose sinks, faucets, and light fixtures that convey artistry through functionality; forego items with unnecessary frills because they typically convey a more formal attitude.

Adding a three-bulb light fixture above the peninsula, *top* lights up the kitchen at night and on dark days. The fixture doubles as a pot rack.

A custom-made linoleum rug *above* softens the hardwood floor and ties the wall color and main countertop color together. The striped rug wipes clean with a damp cloth. A similar rug warms the floor beneath the new dining table *opposite*. (For instructions on making a linoleum floorcloth see page 166.)

undercabinet lighting systems plug into existing wall outlets and attach to cabinet bottoms with screws. If outlets are limited choose an undermount fixture with additional outlets built into the light bar. Before the update the only fixture in this kitchen was a two-bulb sconce above the sink. To bring in more welcoming light, the designers added a second ceiling-mount fixture that also serves as a pot rack and a visual focal point. The classically styled fixture illuminates the peninsula work surface while offering additional storage.

Maximize the beauty of natural light by using only minimal window treatments, such as classic sheer curtain panels or simple light-filtering shades that can be pulled open and out of the way. Prior to the remodel

wooden shutters blocked a great deal of natural light in this space and couldn't be fully opened due to furniture and cabinetry placement. Now lightweight paisley panels allow in light and dress the window in style.

BETTER SEATING

As Kristan did in the kitchen eating area *opposite,* bring living room beauty to the kitchen with fabrics, pillows, candles, and flowers. Ensure comfort for visitors with easy-going dining chairs or a cushion-topped bench. Or if you eat most of your meals at an island or bar, replace your underutilized table with a pair of club chairs that invites relaxation. For more innovative ways to give your kitchen a fresh new face, turn the page.

To see dozens of kitchens **decorated in a variety of styles**, visit *HGTV.com/designers*

A thrift store table and long wooden bench provide room for multiple guests and are arranged so kitchen occupants can easily converse with the cook. New wicker baskets fill the empty space on the microwave cart and offer storage for linens and seasonal accessories.

COSMETIC LIFT

Just as accessories make an outfit, cosmetic changes update a kitchen. Give your kitchen a pulled-together look like the kitchen on pages 116–119 by including a few of these decorating mainstays.

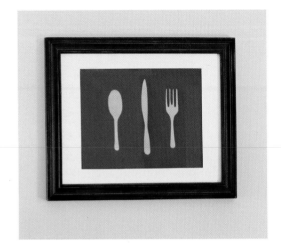

PRETTY PICTURES Because of limited wall space, artwork *left* is often overlooked in many kitchen schemes. Instead of leaving it out, look for new places to add it, such as on the end of an island or along the backsplash. Framed posters, family photos, and botanical prints are excellent options.

CLASSIC FURNISHINGS Because the kitchen is one of the most popular gathering areas in the home, furnish it as stylishly as you would the living room or den. Add a chair and ottoman to an empty corner and dress dining chairs with pillows and cushions for added comfort *below*. Give cabinets a fine furniture look by adding corbels, moldings, and glass doors.

WINDOW DRESSINGS Decorative hooks hold sheer tab-top fabric panels *below* and offer a glimpse of the white-painted window frame. For a dramatic style statement, add colorful valances, swags, and jabots; upholstered or wooden cornices; or interior awnings to the windows in your kitchen. (For more information on kitchen window treatments, see pages 98–99.)

CABINET JEWELS

CHANGING CABINETRY HARDWARE is one of the easiest ways to update your cabinets. To find affordable handles, designer Kristan Cunningham shops at small local hardware stores. "If you're updating a small kitchen, the neighborhood retailers usually have enough handles on hand to complete the project, and most of their selections are reasonably priced," she says. If they don't have what you need, extend your search to larger home centers and the Internet. "If I search long enough, I can usually find the size of handles I want in the price range and style I need," Kristan explains.

HANDLES for this kitchen cost less than $5 each, enabling Kristan to update all the cabinets for just $137. "To use existing drill holes, you'll need to choose hardware that is the same size as what you currently have," she explains. "The existing cabinetry already has holes drilled for 3-inch handles so we chose handles to fit those holes." If you want to change the size of the handles, fill in the existing holes with wood putty and paint over them, or cover the holes with metal backplates that fit behind the new handles.

COLORFUL FABRICS Cabinetry angles and hard surfaces give a kitchen a more linear look than the other gathering spaces in your home, but fabrics can help soften these lines. Toss a few pillows on a bench, twist a tablecloth into a runner, and line the breadbasket with a colorful cotton print to bring living room comfort into this functional space. Handmade throw pillows cushion wooden chair backs, and tieback curtain panels mellow crisp window casings *above*.

WASHABLE RUGS Rugs add color and comfort to all hard surface floors. Choose washable fabric rugs or make a painted floorcloth or a linoleum rug as shown *right*. (To learn how to make a linoleum rug, see page 166.)

PERSONAL REFLECTIONS

Does your kitchen reflect what you love and the way you live? If not give it a new attitude with a few easy changes.

Surface changes, such as a new aluminum backsplash, matching cabinetry hardware, a hard-surface window treatment, and a decorative curtain that separates the kitchen from an office cubby, give this kitchen lots of flash for little cash.

Contemporary metal shelves *right* serve as both storage and display space. A new wooden counter tops a half-wall and provides a spot for buffet service. Khaki-green paint on the walls brings warm color into the once-cool space.

SURFACE CHANGES make a dull kitchen sparkle. If your kitchen lacks the gleam of your own personality, take cues from this *Design on a Dime* makeover, where Kristan Cunningham, Spencer Anderson, and Dave Sheinkopf transformed this once-basic space into a personal showcase for $1,000.

SPLASHY BACKSPLASHES

Is your backsplash less than attractive? Prior to the makeover, the backsplash in this kitchen was a dark faux brick. To give it a new look, Kristan covered the faux brick with aluminum laminate purchased from a countertop supply store. The sleek covering gives the kitchen an industrial touch that underscores the owner's decorating taste. If your backsplash needs a boost on the style charts, you can also coat the area with chalkboard paint or adorn it with a collection of identically framed prints. (For information on how to tile a backsplash, see pages 172–173.)

FLASHY DISPLAYS

As with the aluminum backsplash, new brushed-metal display shelves in the breakfast area reflect an appreciation for clean, industrial-style lines. Drinking glasses purchased from a local import store adorn the shelves and come into service when the owner entertains.

Because kitchens are natural gathering spots, they serve as an ideal place to display art. But you don't need to make a large investment: Contemporary prints in this kitchen are made from a favorite fabric stapled to the back of rectangular corkboard. The colors in the fabric

Prior to its *Design on a Dime* makeover, this kitchen *below* was a flashback to the 1970s. A few simple changes provide some contemporary shine.

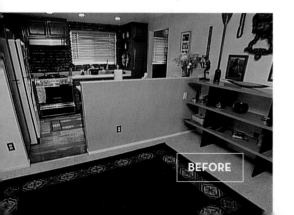

BEFORE

A new green cafe table *above*, made from layers of concentric circles cut from medium-density fiberboard (MDF), combines with new barstools to create an intimate dining spot. A round rug mimics the shape of the table and a new window porthole. For instructions on how to make this table, see pages 164–165.

complement the upholstered furnishings in the adjacent living area.

A curtain panel made from the same fabric used on the art boards provides visual separation between the kitchen work core and an adjacent office cubby. The textural contrast between the twig-print fabric, the shiny shelves, and the drywall finish makes the area a decorative focal point.

FURNITURE POLISH

Before the makeover the owner of the condominium avoided purchasing a table for the breakfast area because he couldn't find one to suit his tastes. The custom-made cafe table *left* and on page 122 matches the owner's requirement for a contemporary yet intimate eating spot. Another bonus: The table doesn't interfere with traffic flow from the kitchen work core to the adjoining living area. (For project instructions, see page 164–165.) For more ways to personalize a kitchen, turn the page.

Originally devoid of furnishings, the breakfast area *left* is now a favorite place for entertaining friends. A new shelf matching the countertop buffet bar steps down a few inches and wraps around the adjacent corner, increasing serving capacity. A metal post gives the shelf additional support and fits the industrial look. New fabric on the cushions creates a custom touch on inexpensive barstools.

Half-round jigsaw cutouts in a pair of aluminum laminate panels fit together to form a contemporary window treatment *above*. The porthole shape ties the kitchen work core to the breakfast area decor and keeps the focus on the view rather than on the wall of a neighboring condo.

The fabric matches the new custom-made art pieces and the curtain panel *left*.

CONTEMPORARY STYLE FOR A SONG

GIVE YOUR KITCHEN a cutting-edge, contemporary look—without doling out a lot of cash—by incorporating a few of these easy decorating ideas:

DECLUTTER. Clear off the countertops and simplify displays to create a more clean-lined look without any expense.

CURVES. Soften crisp edges by tossing in a few affordable curves, such as a dining table with a round glass top, curved-back dining chairs, and a round throw rug.

METALS. Add shiny metal accents by installing inexpensive stainless-steel or nickel knobs and metal display shelves.

FABRIC. Choose affordable cottons or faux suedes in solids or low-key patterns and use them in unpretentious decorative treatments you can make yourself, such as a chair cushion cover or a simple curtain panel.

PERSONAL STAMP

You, your family, and your guests will feel at ease in a kitchen that reflects your personality. Here are a few easy ways to express personal taste through artistic displays.

WINDOW ART If you don't want to inhibit the view out the window, frame it with open shelves. In the kitchen *above* narrow shelves installed between adjacent window frames show off a collection of pitchers. If you lack space along the sides of your window, top it with a shelf valance. (For more window treatment ideas, see pages 98–99.)

CREATING DISPLAY SPACE

CREATING ADDITIONAL display areas in your kitchen can be as simple as adding a home-built plate rack (see page 93) or a few shelves to an open wall *below left*. If storage space is at a premium, put items you use every day on display, including plates, mugs, and glasses. You can also expand your display space by replacing solid cabinet doors with glass-inset doors. Or remove the cabinet doors and fill the holes where the hinges once were with wood putty. Coat the interiors of open cabinets with a contrasting color of paint to set off the items you plan to display. In the kitchen *below right* the space once occupied by an appliance is filled with storage cubbies. For extra pizzazz the interiors are painted one color and the front trim boards are in a contrasting color. Each cubby houses a tall rectangular basket that can be used to store dry goods, veggies, or linens.

PERSONAL COLLECTIONS Display personal collections in your kitchen to add design charm and to tell your own story. Look high and low for display spaces. Open shelves in the island *left* hold colorful serving dishes and matching table linens. In the kitchen *above* wall space near the ceiling line provides display space for colorful prints. A new glass shelf attached to the sink window frame shows off a row of colorful vases.

Moving the sink down a few feet to the right of its original location provides enough wall space on the left side of the sink for a professional range with two ovens, a favorite feature of the owners, who love to bake. Building the refrigerator into the back wall of the kitchen makes the elongated space seem wider.

NATURAL CONNECTION

Fill your kitchen with natural materials and surfaces to experience the artistry of nature from inside your home.

A warming drawer tucked below the microwave *right* makes it easy to keep dinner hot for late arrivals.

NATURE'S BEAUTY BRINGS a sense of warmth and grace to a kitchen. From smooth woods and stones to earthy textures and colors, natural materials entice guests to come in and enjoy. This kitchen—renovated on *Designers' Challenge* by chosen designer Ali Amani—serves as a stunning example of how to warm a room with a variety of natural elements.

WOOD

To make your kitchen feel as friendly and inviting as this one, choose cherry or maple

Before the remodel the all-white kitchen *below* lacked warmth and coziness and did not reflect the owner's taste for earth-inspired design.

cabinets stained a medium or light honey hue or a reddish tone. When combined with a warm stain color, the fine graining in these woods brings a sense of coziness to a room without overpowering the other decorative elements. In this kitchen a hand-rubbed cinnamon finish warms the cherry cabinets. A mahogany dining table extends the warmth of the wood to the breakfast area.

The floors in this kitchen are porcelain tile with a stone look. Oak and maple planks also make a popular choice for kitchens decorated with natural elements because wood is durable and comfortable underfoot.

STONE

Smooth, cool stone creates a look of elegance and tactility. When used on the countertop, stone is both functional and decorative, melding toughness and dependability with sleek sophistication. On the floor stone looks timeless and graceful and is virtually wear-proof. Here natural granite counters bring pattern and sparkle into the room.

BEFORE

These custom-built cabinets *above* offer storage space for cookbooks and serving pieces. The mossy-green granite top provides buffet service for a crowd and can withstand the heat of baking dishes and casseroles just out of the oven.

Raising the ceiling and removing the cabinetry bulkhead makes the kitchen *above* more voluminous while allowing in more light from the original skylight windows. Sheer Roman shades bring welcome texture to the windows and complement the varying wood tones of the mahogany table. Metal slats, leather seats, and mahogany frames make the dining chairs as attractive as they are comfortable.

Handblown glass pendants *right* illuminate the tabletop and bring out the colors in the granite. Handmade metal pulls *far right* are used on both the doors and drawers; they create a visual connection between the stainless-steel appliances and the cabinetry.

COLOR AND TEXTURE

Colors and textures commonly found in nature are the perfect complement to any kitchen with earthy connections. Sage green, sunny yellow, and cattail brown are natural companions, as are sky blue and slate gray. (For advice for choosing a color scheme, see pages 114–115.) The cheerful yellow walls in this kitchen are coated with Venetian plaster, a centuries-old finish that involves mixing ground stone into plaster and then layering the plaster on and sanding it off to create a finish that resembles smooth stone. The ceilings feature the same Venetian plaster finish, but in a slightly lighter shade of yellow.

Hand-hammered pewter pulls create textural variation against the smooth cherry cabinets. Sheer Roman shades control sunlight and are made from loosely woven flax, a natural material that complements the earthy emphasis in this kitchen.

NATURAL LIGHT AND VIEWS

One of the most effective ways to connect your kitchen to nature is to maximize views and sunlight. To accomplish that goal in this kitchen, Ali removed the bulkhead and raised the ceiling 12 inches. The additional height ushers in more light from the existing tall windows, French doors, and the skylight area, which was nearly blocked from view in the original lower-ceiling kitchen. To increase sunlight and views in your kitchen, increase the size of the windows, replace a solid door with a glass model, or replace opaque window treatments with sheer options.

For ways to dress your tabletop with nature-inspired elements, turn the page.

NATURAL STYLE

PAY HOMAGE to this style by filling your kitchen with elements found in nature.

NATURAL SURFACES, such as wood floors, stained (not painted) cabinets, and stone counters, are musts.

A COLOR PALETTE derived from nature also creates the feeling of the great outdoors from inside a room.

EARTH-INSPIRED TEXTURES that fit this style include natural-weave baskets, hand-hammered metals, and woven fabrics such as cotton, linen, and wool.

Extending the granite the full height of the backsplash *above* draws attention to its pattern and color. Insets of decorative glass tiles create more visual interest. For additional backsplash treatment suggestions, see pages 144–145.

TEMPTING TABLETOPS

Whether you're a nature lover like the owners of the kitchen on pages 128–131 or a color enthusiast, your kitchen will benefit from a thoughtfully decorated table.

TABLESCAPES When propped with life's little pleasures, a table becomes a personal gallery to be seen and savored by others. Though compositions can consist of just about anything, your tablescape will be most intriguing if it includes at least one unexpected element, such as a fruit bowl filled with corks and lemons and a dinner plate topped with a bud vase *above*.

DOUBLE-DUTY TABLE A table in the kitchen doesn't have to be reserved for eating. This narrow console *below* is used for display, but it can be pulled into service for buffet-style dining. Garden flowers, a potted plant, and a pillar candle create a simple vignette in front of the large French poster.

CHEERY CHAIRS
Because chairs frame the table, they need to be dressed as well as the tabletop. In this eating area *left* stains in vibrant colors cover the wooden chairs, and colorful place mats and denim napkins adorn the tabletop.

GIVE YOUR TABLETOP a personal look by using table linens in unusual ways.

INSTEAD OF COVERING the entire table with a cloth, twist it down the middle and then dot the folds with candlesticks and bud vases.

LARGE, SQUARE NECK SCARVES also make great table coverings. Place the scarf on the diagonal so the points hang along the sides of the table instead of lining up with the corners. For more drama layer a sheer scarf on top of a solid one.

FOR THE LOOK OF A TABLE RUNNER without the expense, place a row of color-coordinated napkins down the center of the table, lining them up corner-to-corner instead of side-to-side to create a diamond-shape design.

ALWAYS ON DISPLAY When dinner is over don't leave the table bare. Dress it up again with items planned for the next meal's fare, such as stacks of pretty plates and napkins, bowls of fruits for snacking, or bagels stacked inside a clear glass cake stand. A wicker charger topped with sweet peas in bud vases and ripe green apples *above* create a fresh, colorful display.

KEEP IT SIMPLE Displays don't have to be complex to be appreciated. A plant growing from a bright red urn and a few cheerful linens *right* bring color and whimsy into this breakfast area.

A huge, two-tiered granite-top center island melds form with function in this stylish kitchen. Hand-rubbed painted and glazed cabinets, intricate molding treatments, and professional-quality appliances complete the look.

FLUENT FRENCH

If you want your kitchen to look sophisticated yet feel cozy and casual, infuse it with a fresh French country ambience.

ORIGINATING IN THE SUNNY
hillsides of rural France, French country
style includes components such as old-
fashioned fixtures and antique-looking
cabinets that fit as well in humble
farmhouses as they do in elegant homes.
To create this time-proven look, use some
of the following style elements in your
kitchen. For more ways to add French
flavor see pages 138–139.

NATURAL BEAUTY

For an authentic French country look, let
nature guide your kitchen design through
a selection of natural surfaces, a classic
color scheme, and carved wooden details.

Apothecary drawers and beaded-board drawer accents give the built-in cabinets *above* the look of freestanding furniture. Hand-hammered metal handles and old-fashioned seed glass add vintage charm—which was previously lacking in this kitchen *left*. Ropelike moldings lend a traditional touch to the upper cabinet moldings. A professional-grade cooktop and range create a stylish look while increasing cooking function.

The adjacent family room media center features the same classic furniture detailing as the kitchen. The new open layout encourages family gatherings and enables guests to mingle without getting in the cook's way.

Common flooring choices for this decorating style appear time-worn and include salvaged or distressed wood planks, rustic terra-cotta tiles, and honed stone. Similarly traditional countertops of wood, stone, or tile suit the style well. Here golden granite covers the counters and backsplash, and earthy bamboo planks cover the floor. Popular color schemes recall the past and feature soft and faded tones, such as creams, golden honey, and grayed blue—as shown in this kitchen—or deep, rich hues like cranberry, navy, and forest green.

Heirloom-looking cabinets often look like freestanding furniture and may feature a hand-rubbed painted and glazed finish—as in this kitchen—or a natural wood tone finish. Intricate molding treatments, decorative corbels, and beaded-board panels are also common to the style and accentuate the fine furniture look. Large farmhouse tables, with a waxed or low-sheen stained wood finish, and chairs that might include carved details with woven rush or padded seats complement the style because of their casual appeal.

OLD AND NEW

The beauty of any vintage-style kitchen is the ease with which you can mix and match old and new. The farm table and chairs *opposite* and most of the accessories were part of the original kitchen—and they look even better in the newly remodeled space. Bronzed-metal barstools, shown on page 134, are new, but their ornate design makes them a perfect fit in this space. The iron chandelier is a newly purchased antique.

FABRICS AND ACCESSORIES

Provençal fabrics feature a variety of 19th-century botanical motifs that mix well with country stripes, checks, and solid fabrics in matching or contrasting colors. Yellow or gold is often paired with red, green, or blue. The floral fabric on the dining chair cushions was the owners' inspiration for this entire kitchen transformation. To give the fabric even more prominence, *Designers' Challenge* chosen designer Brian Klaas had canisters, shown on page 135, and a bowl, shown on page 138, painted to match.

Complete your accessorizing with baskets, wrought-iron fixtures, vintage collectibles, and fresh flowers. These items will make your room come alive with color, personality, and French country flavor. For more ways to instill French flavor in your kitchen, turn the page.

Reproduction faucets *top* lend an old-fashioned look. Single-hand controls provide modern functionality.

Cabinetry panels disguise the refrigerator *above* and the dishwashers, ensuring the French country style of the kitchen is the center of attention.

FRENCH FLAVOR

Include some of these stylish elements—from the kitchen featured on pages 134–137—in your kitchen to build a French country theme.

MIX AND MATCH COLLECTIBLES French country collectibles are available in a variety of colors and patterns at flea markets, accessory shops, and antiques stores. For instance you may find gold, olive green, or French blue plates and earth-tone table linens to set off textured baskets, iron candlesticks, and pottery pitchers. The new bowl *left* was painted to match the owners' favorite French fabric.

FABRICS WITH COUNTRY FLAVOR The floral fabric shown on the table *right* was the owners' design inspiration for this kitchen; the soft colors and romantic floral motif help define the French country styling. To begin your kitchen design with a focal-point fabric, search fabric stores for a color combination and pattern that illustrate a look you love. Then have paint colors custom-mixed to complement the fabric.

BEADED BOARD AND CORBELS Welcome back yesteryear with traditional details such as intricately carved corbels *above left*, arches and raised panel doors *above center left*, and beaded board *left*. Many of these furniture details are available ready-made from home centers and can be installed in just a few hours.

ECLECTIC BEAUTY

If you love all things beautiful, regardless of style, genre, or era, eclecticism may be the decor for you.

Removing the wall between the family room and kitchen provided enough space for a center island, now a favorite gathering space in the home and the primary work area. Sleek, contemporary brushed-metal barstools are ergonomically designed to provide comfort for hours. No detail forgotten, a niche on the far end of the island provides a discreet spot for pet dishes.

Contemporary pendant lights fitted with full-spectrum lightbulbs *right* cast a golden glow on the island work surface. Red-painted walls offset favorite framed prints.

THE BROADER YOUR TASTES in food, hobbies, and clothing, the more likely you are to embrace an eclectic look. Mixing and matching is the mantra in this kitchen style; elements come from different periods and places. The primary selection criterion comes from the heart—if you love it, buy it, because in this design philosophy you'll likely find a way to make it work.

The key to pulling a collection of attractive yet unrelated pieces together is to find or create some commonality in each element. In this kitchen *Designers' Challenge* chosen designer Bette Hornstein creates unity by way of a warm, welcoming color scheme, clean-lined fixtures and cabinetry, and a casual ambience. Equally as effective eclectic connections can be made through a design that displays a neutral or other easy-to-identify color

palette, a higher degree of design complexity among the cabinetry and furnishings, or through a more formal attitude. Here's how these unifying principles work.

COLOR CONNECTION

The easiest and most cost effective way to bring cohesion to varying design elements is through color. In this kitchen the fabric that makes up the awning-style window valances creates a visual tie between the honey tones of the cabinetry and the rustic red wall color. An inlaid strip of purple heartwood (which actually appears red) relates the oak floor to the cabinets and the fabric. Additional color connections can be created through the use of color-matched knobs, table linens, throw rugs, upholstery, and pottery.

BEFORE

Prior to its *Designers' Challenge* remodeling, this all-white cottage kitchen *left* did not reflect the vivacious personality of the owner. Chosen designer Bette Hornstein transformed the kitchen into a charming gathering space that showcases the eclectic taste of the owner.

Polished gold-tone granite *above* sparkles against rustic red walls and honey-color cabinets. A leftover piece of granite becomes an attractive cutting board that holds a few of the owner's polished silver collectibles.

Made from birch the grainlike appearance of the cabinets *above* is actually a striated painted finish that mimics the finish on a favorite chair in the adjoining family room. Windows are original to the room; leaving them in their existing location helped keep the budget in check. Using glass doors on the cabinet between the windows retains the open look of the window wall while providing more storage and display space.

ECLECTIC STYLE An eclectic style enables you to mix what you love—from classic pieces you've inherited to quirky contemporary finds—to create your personal look. The only design requirement is to find a common element among your collections, such as earthy textures, angular or curvaceous shapes, or pastel or primary colors. These visual connectors will unify your design and give your eclectic scheme a more cohesive look.

For more information on **eclectic style**, visit *HGTV.com/designstyles*

Though a wall was torn down, the owner has more storage and display space than ever before. The designer's conscientious space planning put every inch of space to work, including creating a narrow display niche by the refrigerator and adding more cabinets to the kitchen wall on the opposite side of the dining room entrance.

Fabric valances complement the clean lines of the cabinetry *right*. Fabric colors visually tie walls, floors, and countertops together. Moving the refrigerator to the opposite side of the room makes the appliance convenient to both the dining room and work core.

DESIGN COMPLEXITY

The cabinets selected for this kitchen are Shaker style, an old-fashioned, unpretentious facade that appears as comfortable in a rural farmhouse as it does in this urban dwelling. The barstools, fixtures, and hardware convey a much more contemporary attitude, but because all these elements are simple the combination makes for a compatible mix. If furniture details and ornate carvings are your favorite cabinetry features, choose chairs, hardware, and accessories that also have a few more intricate accents.

ALL IN THE ATTITUDE

Another easy way to create design cohesion is through casual or formal ambience. In this kitchen the cabinets, window treatments, and collections all have an easy-going appearance that makes it possible to mix ceramic roosters and vintage crocks with contemporary pendant lights. For ways to instill design dash in often overlooked backsplashes, turn the page.

SPLASHES OF STYLE

Bring more color, texture, and style into your kitchen with a backsplash treatment as attractive as these—and the one featured on pages 140–143.

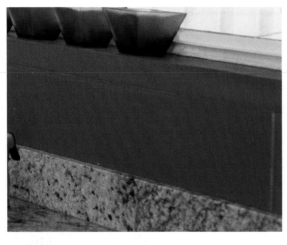

CLEARLY VISIBLE In the kitchen featured on pages 140–143, a layer of glass protects the red-painted backsplash *above*. The solution also works well for wallpapered and faux-finish backsplash treatments.

CONCRETE THINKING The orange and yellow backsplash tiles *below* are made from stained concrete. Larger concrete tiles cover the countertops. Both types of tiles accentuate the stain colors of the cabinets. Staining the concrete brings out hairline cracks, pores, and texture common in concrete, yet the surface is smooth and durable. A sealant renders the concrete resistant to water and most stains. The honed surface looks equally as attractive against a solid-color countertop made from solid surfacing or natural stone.

GLASS GLOW A combination of ceramic and glass mosaic tiles give this backsplash *above left* a fun and funky look. The reflective qualities of the glass create interesting contrast between the ceramic tiles and the granite countertop. To make glass backsplash tiles "pop" even more, place them against a shiny white or stainless-steel countertop. If your kitchen connects to an exterior wall, select a backsplash made of glass block that filters in the sunlight as shown *below left* and on page 91. The material comes in a variety of patterns to complement most cabinetry and countertop designs.

STONE EXTENSION Polished granite extends from the countertop to the wall cabinets in this ageless kitchen. Installed in slabs, there are very few seams and no grout lines. For more contrast use a complementary stone on one of the two adjoining surfaces. For more visual connection top the island with the same pattern used on the backsplash.

The owners purchased stainless-steel appliances prior to the remodeling, so interior designer Sandra Wisot selected rich sable-stained alderwood cabinetry to set off the shiny metal facades.

MEDITERRANEAN EXPRESSIONS

Your house may tell you what style to select for the kitchen. This one speaks of a vintage Spanish legacy.

A convection oven on top and a conventional oven below provide baking options in the remodeled kitchen *right*.

LOADED WITH PERIOD DETAILS, this 1928 Spanish revival-style house captured the owners' hearts. Almost all the rooms, especially the breakfast room (see page 151), are favorite spots. The kitchen, however, was less compelling.

Before the remodeling the work core lacked a cohesive layout, and the look didn't match the house at all, with elements such as a vinyl floor, white tile countertops, track lighting from the 1970s, and lackluster oak cabinetry. A large window over the sink—though it allowed in sun—was a dated design as well.

An adjacent laundry room promised loads of potential space if it could merge with the existing kitchen; however, a load-bearing wall stood in the way. Removing the wall and shoring up the structure with a special beam allowed the two spaces to combine as one.

INSPIRED DECISIONS

The owners' earlier purchase of new stainless-steel appliances drove some of the decisions made by the chosen *Designers' Challenge* interior designer Sandra Wisot. Existing details throughout the house provided additional design guidance, inspiring the selection of kitchen materials and elements that harmonize with the prevailing Mediterranean flavor.

To suit this house, sable-stained alderwood cabinets establish an air of richness, posing the perfect complement to the stainless-steel appliances. Crown moldings, clean-lined recessed panels on doors, and elegant satin-nickel hardware speak to the fine craftsmanship found throughout the rest of the house.

Terra-cottalike ceramic tiles selected for the backsplashes—and larger, lighter versions for the floor—offer variations in

BEFORE

Before remodeling the kitchen *left* sported a vinyl floor and white tile counters that didn't suit the Spanish style of the home.

A clipped corner *above* invites shelves for display and cookbooks. The colorful vase and woven basket fit the Spanish style.

MORE FOR YOUR BUDGET

SANDRA WISOT, CID, the chosen designer for this *Designers' Challenge* project, strives to give her clients the features they want. "Very often," she says, "when we meet a client, we find that they have wonderful ideas that cost a little bit more than their budget allows. So it becomes a challenge to produce the desired effect in other ways. Perhaps we'll change fabrics or we'll do some adjustment of the materials in order to please everyone."

To make your kitchen budget go further without sacrificing great style, try these ideas. (For information about what common kitchen features cost, turn to page 179.)

MAKE OVER EXISTING CABINETRY. If your cabinets are sturdy, give them a fresh look with new hardware, moldings, and paint. (To learn if your cabinets can be saved, turn to page 51.) Another option is to purchase stock cabinetry (as opposed to more expensive semicustom or custom cabinetry) and perk up the look with moldings and paint.

KEEP THE SINK NEAR ITS ORIGINAL LOCATION. Relocating plumbing lines can be costly. However, if your sink isn't efficient in its current location, it's worth the money to make the move. Find ways to cut the budget elsewhere.

SUBSTITUTE SOLID GRANITE FOR GRANITE TILES. Solid granite slabs are typically more expensive than thinner granite tiles. Opt for tiles and you'll enjoy the permanence and beauty of the product, but for less investment.

USE SMALL DOSES OF EXPENSIVE FABRIC. You can have that $50 per yard fabric if you limit its usage. Buy only a yard or two and use it to make pillows for a banquette or to cover chair seats. Fill out your decorating needs with more affordable fabrics.

SHOP WHOLESALE OUTLETS AND FACTORY DIRECT. Frequent these venues to find attractive kitchen fixtures and fittings as well as surfacing materials at a discount.

PURCHASE DISCONTINUED PRODUCTS. Just about any type of store you visit—fabric store, home improvement center, or tile dealer—will place discontinued or slightly damaged products on sale. Ask if these types of products are available and be courageous in your bargaining.

WORK IN PHASES. Take your time remodeling your kitchen and you can pay as you go, stretching the budget over several months or even years.

Merging the former laundry room with the kitchen allows space for a desk area and additional storage. The end of this cabinet run hides a litter box for the owners' three cats and a place for food and water bowls.

Across from the desk area, this bank of cabinetry conceals the washer and dryer.

color that one might find in an authentic Mediterranean Spanish kitchen.

Dakota mahogany granite countertops repeat the tones found in the cabinets as well as the backsplash and flooring. This provides a unifying visual feature and suits the era of the house perfectly.

All the materials continue into the former laundry room, which is now open to the kitchen, providing a desk area, additional storage, and matching cabinet doors that conceal the washer and dryer in attractive Mediterranean style.

Today the kitchen's style fits the house as well as the adjoining breakfast room did from the beginning, assuring an uninterrupted atmosphere of Mediterranean magic.

If you're searching for ideas for your breakfast room or kitchen seating area, turn the page.

If you're searching for ideas for your breakfast room or kitchen seating area, turn the page.

ELEMENTS OF MEDITERRANEAN STYLE

RICH, DARK WOOD

TERRA-COTTA AND/OR SPANISH TILES

IRON SCROLLWORK

WEATHERED FINISHES

EARTHY HUES with touches of red, if desired.

For more information on **Mediterranean style**, visit *HGTV.com/designstyles*

The L-shape leg of this kitchen is space gained from the old laundry room. The additional windows help brighten the kitchen.

These backsplash tiles *above* offer all the variations of authentic terra-cotta tiles but ensure the easy-clean characteristics of ceramic tile.

SITTING PRETTY

The kitchen on pages 146–149 adjoins a breakfast room for enjoying meals. Whether you want to eat in the kitchen or nearby, incorporate stylish seating ideas such as these into your plans.

ISLAND SEATING Extend an island countertop to create an overhang that invites a row of stools, as shown *left*. This kitchen also opens to the breakfast room, where a large table and chairs offer additional seating options.

TRESTLE TABLE Play up a kitchen with heirloom character by adding a trestle table, such as the one *below*, and chairs charmingly personalized in chalk.

BANQUETTE One of the best ways to squeeze additional seating into a tight kitchen space is to build a banquette along a wall and pull up a table beside it. This handsome traditional-style cushioned bench *above* slips in beneath the window for a sunny setting.

BREAKFAST ROOM Just off the new kitchen featured on pages 146–149, this sunny breakfast room *below* is the favorite space of one of the owners. Abundant windows and an attractive built-in cabinet make it easy to see why.

TABLE-HEIGHT COUNTER You can integrate a table-height counter on one side of your island. This rounded version *above* seats three comfortably and features the same brilliant blue granite countertop as the island.

SITTING AREA If a table and chairs don't offer the kind of kitchen comfort you're seeking, replace them with a love seat or two. In the kitchen *right* the owners turned their seldom-used breakfast room into a sitting area.

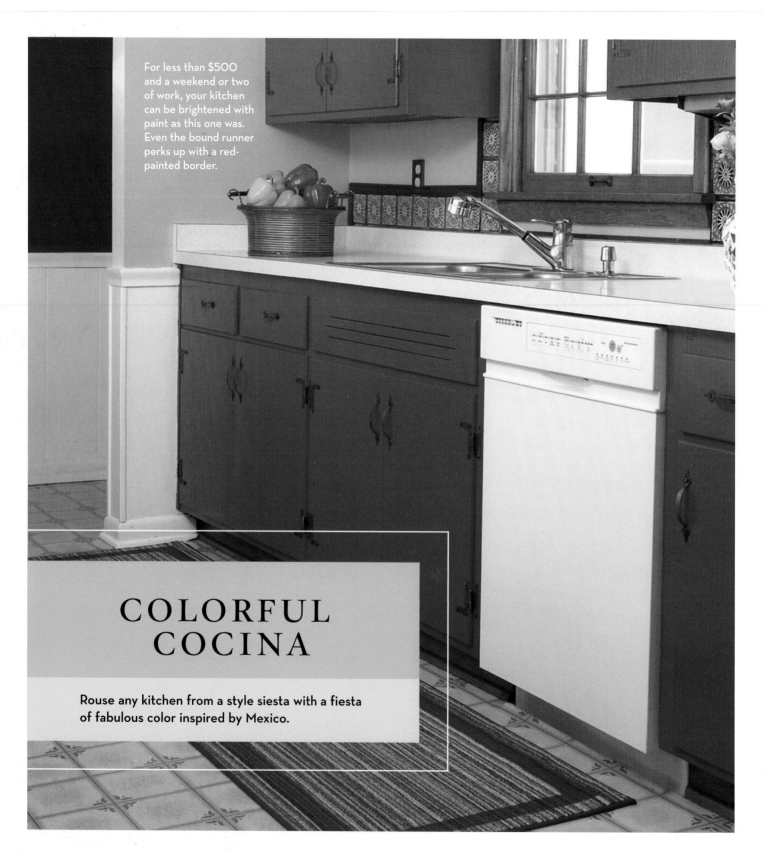

For less than $500 and a weekend or two of work, your kitchen can be brightened with paint as this one was. Even the bound runner perks up with a red-painted border.

COLORFUL COCINA

Rouse any kitchen from a style siesta with a fiesta of fabulous color inspired by Mexico.

UNDERSTATED DECORATING works well in the bedroom, but the kitchen is one room in the house that can benefit from a livelier look—and sleepy surroundings just won't do. This kitchen *below* functioned well but needed a pick-me-up to erase dull wood cabinets and plain walls. In addition a low light-box-style fixture consumed the entire ceiling and left the space feeling cramped and dated. The adjoining breakfast area needed freshening too.

If the current style in your kitchen and breakfast area is more akin to siesta than fiesta, consider the wake-up strategy used by interior designer Barbara Sculati for this *Decorating Cents* makeover. Her primary goal: Lavish the kitchen in colors that reflect the heritage of one of the homeowners and create a spirited environment for a family to gather.

LIQUID ASSETS

One of the most affordable and effective decorating tools you can invest in is paint. If your kitchen cabinets are sturdy but lackluster, paint provides a dramatic

Tiles made in Mexico *right* gave this makeover a good place to begin the color selections. Turn to page 157 to learn the secret of installing similar tiles so you can remove them or move them on a whim.

transformation for little money. (For tips on painting cabinets, turn to page 154.) Begin by choosing the palette: Use one element as color inspiration, such as a platter or fabric. In this case new Mexican tiles purchased for the backsplash result in a cheerful selection of sunny yellow for the kitchen walls, rich red for the cabinetry, and cobalt blue for an adjoining hallway. For contrast the breakfast room cabinetry freshens up in crisp white.

The transforming power of paint goes beyond walls and cabinets, however. Use paint to tie other elements to the decor. A runner for the kitchen and an area rug for the breakfast room, for example, each receive a spray-painted red border as a visual link to the cabinetry. The dining table joins the theme with a red-painted border on the tabletop (see *opposite below* page 155). Even the old dining chandelier earns a redo with white spray paint and a new drum-style shade in white.

Before remodeling *left* there was nothing notable about this sleepy kitchen and breakfast room.

BEFORE

Track lighting might be one of the most affordable lighting replacements around. This entire fixture *above* cost about $60.

GLASS ACTS

INCORPORATE COLOR on unexpected elements to add inexpensive finishing touches to your kitchen. Interior designer Barbara Sculati starts with clear glass pieces—chandelier crystals and cordial drinking glass—to spice this space with more color. To bring this window treatment *bottom* home, drape a square of embroidered fabric over a tension rod as a valance. Then add sparkle with colored-glass chandelier crystals suspended from cup hooks screwed into the bottom edge of the fascia board. Colored glass accents continue in the breakfast area *below* and *opposite*, where glass votives step into the scheme. To transform clear glass with color, use spray paint *below left* formulated for glass (sometimes called stained-glass spray paint). Use chains *below right* to suspend the votives across a window so sunlight filters through the colored glass by day and light the candles during evenings for a romantic glow.

START TO FINISH

Begin any major kitchen painting project by clearing the room and removing the cabinet doors and drawers. Taking down the huge ceiling fixture in this kitchen revealed that some of the wall-hung cabinet doors had been cut in half to accommodate the drop of the ceiling fixture. Rather than construct new cabinet doors, two of the doorless areas received new shelves and painted interiors for display. For the center opening, adding holiday lights and a translucent panel (see *opposite* and page 157) serves as a creative cover-up. Track lighting replaces the old light box.

While the cabinet doors went back into place in the kitchen, doors on the breakfast room cabinetry remained off to create open shelves for display *opposite*. Lining the shelves with patterned red fabric and adding slipcovers to the new dining chairs—reworked office chairs—complete the makeover with festive flair.

For specifics on refreshing your kitchen with these low-cost strategies, turn the page.

For more information on **Southwestern and South of the Border style**, visit *HGTV.com/designstyles*

SOUTH-OF-THE BORDER STYLE

BRIGHT PRIMARY PAINT COLORS

RUGS AND FABRICS in a similar lively palette

COLORFUL MEXICAN TILES or terra-cotta tiles

ACCESSORIES from Mexico

ART depicting south-of-the-border scenes

PAINT LIKE A PRO

THE SECRET BEHIND A SUCCESSFUL PAINTED FINISH on cabinetry is to use quality primer and paint. Start by removing cabinet doors, drawers, and all the hardware. Lay doors and drawer fronts flat on a protected work surface. Lightly sand the cabinet bodies, the doors, and the drawer fronts. Wipe surfaces clean with a tack cloth. Apply latex primer to all the surfaces, working quickly to avoid ridges caused by wet primer applied over a dry edge; let dry according to the manufacturer's directions. Apply one or more coats of latex paint, again working quickly to avoid ridges; let dry between coats. Rehang cabinetry and hardware.

Taking down the light-box-style fixture revealed that doors on three upper cabinets had been cut in half, leaving the upper portions open. Adding shelves and painting the interiors turns two openings into assets. The third receives a cover up (see page 157).

This space is all about bright color. Painting the hallway blue and the wainscoting white *below* makes the red and yellow in the kitchen even more dramatic. The mosaic frame around the mirror pulls in all the colors.

What a difference a weekend or two can make. Room-refreshing white paint for the shelves and wainscoting and sunny yellow on upper walls bring on a whole new attitude. Spray-paint an old light fixture and finish with a new shade for a total transformation. This fixture in the breakfast room *above* earns a cleaner look with white spray paint and a new white drum-style shade.

155

CHEAP THRILLS FAST

Transform a kitchen and breakfast room in a weekend using the low-cost decorating strategies from the kitchen on pages 152–155.

DINING CHAIR FAST CHANGE

Create affordable seating by recycling inexpensive office chairs. These dining chairs can suit casual and formal dining with two sets of washable slipcovers for quick changes.

1. Unscrew the back from the chair, flip the back upside down, and reattach it using the upper screw holes on the chair back supports **(A)**. This provides a taller, more comfortable backrest for diners.
2. Spray-paint the chair the desired color; let dry.
3. Make pillowcase-style covers for the chair backs **(B)** and matching fabric toppers for the seats **(C)**.

PAINT A RUG For the kitchen and breakfast area, purchase a finished-edge rug. For a custom touch, spray-paint a border around the edges. Here's how to do it yourself:

1. Tape off the border and protect the areas you don't want painted with additional masking tape and kraft paper **(A)**.
2. Spray-paint the border; let dry.
3. Remove the paper and tape **(B)**.

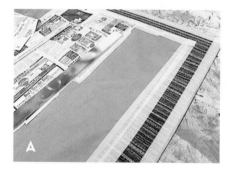

PANEL ILLUSION Use this trick to fill an unwanted opening in a kitchen cabinet, as shown on page 155. Or adapt the idea to a window where you need privacy but want to admit light. This opening gains a moody glow by adding string lights to the interior **(A)**.

1. Fashion a frame for the panel using a wooden shutter with the slats removed, or make your own frame to fit using 2×2s.
2. Have a piece of translucent acrylic cut to fit the opening in the shutter or frame at a home center. Or insert a piece of glass and create the foggy effect using frosted-glass spray paint.
3. To create a decorative border around the frame, paint or stencil a design or glue on decorative paper images. Here reduced color photocopies of Mexican tiles adhere to the frame **(B)** with decoupage medium.

see page 155

LIGHT FANTASTIC

Spray-paint an old light fixture **(A)** and finish with a new shade for a total transformation. The fixture in the breakfast room earns a cleaner look with white spray paint and a new white drum-style shade **(B)**.

TEMPORARY TILE TRICK If you rent your home or you don't want to make the commitment of a tiled backsplash, use designer Barbara Sculati's you-can-take-it-with-you tiling technique:

1. Adhere a square of industrial-strength hook-and-loop tape to the back of each tile **(A)**.
2. Adhere the opposite side of the hook-and-loop tape to the corresponding location on the wall.
3. Press the tile in place **(B)**.

PROJECTS FOR YOUR KITCHEN

Whether you want to save money by doing some of the work yourself, or you're searching for ways to personalize your kitchen, this section of projects can help you achieve both goals. The projects shown on pages 160–167 offer an ideal means for inviting in more color. The rolling cart, message boards, dining table, and linoleum rug projects all promise great style too. Then strap on your tool belt, and turn to pages 168–173 to learn how easy it is to install your own sink and faucet, laminate flooring, and tiled backsplash.

Customize a dresser to meet your needs as a rolling kitchen island. Here one end of the island is outfitted with a paper towel holder and cup hooks for utensils. You could substitute these features for other conveniences, such as open shelves for cookbooks or a wine rack.

MATERIALS

Old, sturdy dresser

Paper towel bar, wood

Water-base primer

Latex paint, in the desired color

12×12-inch ceramic tiles for countertop, white*

Ceramic bullnose tiles for countertop edges, white

Tile adhesive

Grout

Cup hooks

Chalkboard or chalkboard paint applied to hardboard

Molding

Screws

Drawer pulls (optional)

Casters (if desired)

TOOLS

Cordless screwdriver

Fine-grit sandpaper

Tack cloth

Stir stick

Paintbrush

Tile cutter

Trowel (to spread tile adhesive)

Bucket for grout and for rinse water

Rubber-blade grout float

Sponge

*See Step 3. You may wish to use smaller size tiles to avoid cutting tiles to fit.

ROLLING ISLAND

No space for a large island like those shown elsewhere in this book? Dress up a vintage dresser **(A)** and gain an attractive rolling island.

STEP BY STEP

1. Remove the dresser drawers and the pulls or knobs. Smooth surfaces with sandpaper; wipe with a tack cloth. Finish surfaces with primer. Prime the paper towel bar. Let dry.

2. Paint the dresser and paper towel bar in the desired color; let dry. Recoat if needed; let dry.

3. Test-fit the 12×12-inch tiles and bullnose tiles on the dresser top to see if any need to be cut. **Note:** *Adjusting the tile spacing may eliminate the need to make cuts, but keep in mind that grout stains more easily than the tiles themselves. Cut the tiles to size, if needed. (See page 173 for cutting tile.)* **Note:** *If you don't want to invest in a tile cutter, rent one. Or have a tile store or home center make the cuts for you.* Secure the tiles to the dresser top with tile adhesive following the manufacturer's directions. Let the adhesive dry for the amount of time recommended on the packaging.

For more **projects and ideas**, visit *HGTV.com/kitchens*

4. Fill spaces between tiles with grout using a grout float; follow the manufacturer's instructions for drying time. Remove excess grout using a damp sponge.

5. Screw the paper towel bar horizontally on one side of the island. Secure a row of cup hooks below the holder as shown **(B)**.

6. If the back of the dresser is reasonably smooth, finish with primer, let dry, and paint with chalkboard paint. Follow the paint manufacturer's directions for application recommendations and drying times. If the back of the dresser is rough, have a

chalkboard cut to fit and frame with molding to finish. Or paint your own chalkboard on hardboard cut to fit the back; frame the chalkboard with molding to finish **(B)**.

7. Paint the original knobs on the dresser or substitute new or vintage knobs for them. Reinstall. Install casters, if needed.

TOP ALTERNATIVES

IF CERAMIC TILE ISN'T YOUR STYLE, consider these countertop alternatives:

GRANITE OR STONE TILES. Add a ritzy twist to your dressed-up dresser with a surface of granite, marble, slate, or limestone tiles. Look-alike ceramic versions are also available.

MARBLE OR WOOD. Purchase a piece of marble for rolling out dough if you bake a lot of breads and cookies. If you spend much time chopping vegetables, invest in a quality chopping board to cut on. Lay the surfaces directly on top of the painted island or store them in a drawer until you need them.

STAINLESS STEEL. Lend an industrial edge to the island with a stainless-steel top. Make a kraft paper template of the dresser top, noting its depth. Take the template and measurements with you to a metal fabricator and have a stainless-steel "skin" fashioned for the top. Have the "skin" made with preformed edges so you can slip the piece over the countertop edges and grip underneath the wood top so that the stainless steel stays firmly in place.

CHALKBOARD PANEL CABINET

You can renew tired cabinets with paint by introducing refreshing, unexpected colors. But you don't have to stop there: Use specially formulated paint to transform the center panel on ordinary wood cabinets into a fun and useful chalkboard surface.

A

B

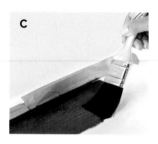

C

MATERIALS

Water-base primer

Latex paint, in white or the color of your choice

Chalkboard paint, green or black

TOOLS

Screwdriver

Fine-grit sandpaper

Tack cloth

Paintbrushes or small foam roller

Stir stick

Low-tack painter's tape

STEP BY STEP

1. Remove the cabinet doors and drawers; also remove knobs, pulls, and hinges. Lightly sand all surfaces **(A)**. Wipe the surfaces clean with a tack cloth.

2. Brush primer onto all surfaces **(B)**; let dry. (If you prefer a smoother finish, use a small foam roller instead of a brush.) Lightly sand the primed surfaces. Wipe with a tack cloth.

3. Using painter's tape mask off any areas, such as the center panel of a door, that you plan to finish with chalkboard paint. Paint the remaining surfaces with the desired base coat color. Let dry. **Note:** *For more complete coverage apply a second coat of paint; let dry.*

4. Mask off any base-coated areas with painter's tape. Brush or roll on the chalkboard paint **(C)**; let dry. Apply additional coats as recommended by the manufacturer. Allow the chalkboard paint to set for the recommended period.

5. Reassemble the cabinets.

Recessed panels in the cabinet are ready-made for applying chalkboard paint.

MAGNETIC MESSAGE BOARD

Create a place to write messages, jot phone numbers, and make a grocery list.

MATERIALS

Wood frame (or 1× lumber to make a frame)

1× lumber for shelf

Perforated board

Thin steel sheet

Construction adhesive

Wood stain or latex paint (optional)

Hanging hardware

TOOLS

Miter box, backsaw (optional)

Table saw

Caulking gun

Stir stick

Paintbrush or foam brush

Rags (if you need to wipe off stain)

Nail gun and nails (or hammer and nails)

STEP BY STEP

1. Purchase a wood frame in the desired size. (Or construct a wood frame from 1× lumber, mitering the board ends using a miter box and backsaw.) Use a table saw to cut a 1× shelf to fit across the inside bottom edge of the frame.

2. Using a table saw, cut a piece of perforated board to fit the frame. Have a home center cut a thin piece of steel slightly smaller than the perforated board, allowing enough room to nail the perforated board to the frame.

3. Apply construction adhesive with a caulking gun to the back of the steel. Secure the steel piece to one side of the perforated board.

4. Stain or paint the frame (or frame pieces) and the shelf piece as desired; let dry.

5. If you are making your own frame, nail the frame pieces together and nail the shelf to the frame. Nail the perforated board to the frame.

6. Secure the hanging hardware to the back of the frame and to the wall and hang the message board.

This clever magnetic message board, featured on an episode of *Design on a Dime*, clears the clutter off the refrigerator. The owners of this kitchen (see pages 116–121) use colorful magnetic letters to leave each other messages. You can also use magnets to display handwritten messages, carryout menus, and phone numbers.

163

MATERIALS

½-inch-thick medium-density
  fiberboard (MDF)

Construction adhesive

Finishing nails or nails designed
  for a nail gun

Water-base primer

Latex paint, in the desired color

Clear water-base polyacrylic

Metal dowels

Clear epoxy

TOOLS

Pencil

Thumbtacks

String

Measuring tape

Jigsaw

Fine-grit sandpaper

Tack cloth

Caulking gun

Hammer or nail gun

Paintbrush

Stir stick

Drop cloth

Drill equipped with a bit to
  match the metal dowels

Plastic bucket

MDF discs, in various sizes, stack up to form the sculptural
base of this bar-height table. You can make the table base
and top almost any size to suit your space. Use the chart
opposite as a guideline for sizing your table.

BUILD A TABLE

If you can cut circles from MDF, apply glue, drive nails, and paint, then you can easily build this *Design on a Dime* table. Spencer Anderson shows how it literally stacks up for style!

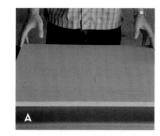

STEP BY STEP

1. Draw different-size circles (including one for the tabletop) onto MDF **(A)**, referring to the chart *below*. To make a compass for drawing circles, push a thumbtack through one end of a length of string and tie a pencil to the opposite end. Push the thumbtack into the MDF, pull the string taut, and use the pencil at the other end of the string to draw a circle. Adjust the length of the string to vary the circle sizes.

2. Cut the circles out using a jigsaw **(B)**. Sand the edges of all the pieces and the tabletop. Wipe away residue with a tack cloth.

3. Apply construction adhesive to the disks **(C)**. Stack the disks **(D)**, nailing them for additional security. Offset the disks as you build up the base, making sure the base remains balanced and stable as you increase the height. **Note:** *Construct the base in two separate sections because MDF is a heavy material and two sections plus the top will be easier to transport into the room.*

4. Prime the two base sections and the tabletop; let dry. Paint the pieces in the desired color; let dry. Coat the base sections with one or two coats of clear water-base polyacrylic; let dry.

5. Protect the floor of the room where you plan to locate the table with a drop cloth. Carry in the two base sections and the tabletop and set them on the drop cloth. Drill into both base halves to accept the metal dowels **(E)**. Hammer dowels into the lower half of the base **(F)**. Apply construction adhesive to the lower half of the base and slip the top section over the dowels.

6. Mix clear epoxy in a plastic bucket, following the manufacturer's instructions. Pour the clear epoxy onto the tabletop **(G)** and spread it to the edges and sides with a paintbrush **(H)**. Allow the epoxy to dry as recommended.

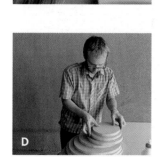

TABLE DIMENSIONS Construct this table to the desired height to serve as a coffee table, dining table, or bar table. The height you decide to make the table will determine how many MDF circles you need to cut. When determining the height of the table remember to account for the thickness of the MDF tabletop.

	DIAMETER	HEIGHT
COFFEE TABLE	36"–42"	15"–17"
DINING	40" minimum (60" seats 5)	28"–30"
BAR HEIGHT	36"–42"	42"
DISCS FOR BASE	7"–18"	

CUT A RUG

Take a cue from *Design on a Dime* designer Kristan Cunningham and fashion a rug from linoleum. You'll gain a surface for your kitchen floor that is colorful, soft underfoot, durable, and easy to clean.

MATERIALS

Linoleum remnant to serve as backing

Water-base adhesive formulated for linoleum tiles

Linoleum tiles (12×12 inch), in the desired color(s)*

¾-inch-wide plastic reducer strips (also called transition moldings)**

TOOLS

Surface for cutting (such as plywood laid across sawhorses or a garage or basement floor)

Measuring tape

Marking pen

Chalk line

Straightedge

Utility knife

Masking tape

Rubber gloves

Trowel

*Size your rug in increments to accommodate full-size 12×12-inch tiles to avoid the extra step of cutting the tiles.

**Reducer strips create a smooth transition from the height of the tiles down to the floor, all the way around the rug.

STEP BY STEP

1. To make the backing for the rug, spread the linoleum remnant flat on a surface that is safe to cut on, such as plywood leaned against a wall **(A)**. Determine how large you want the rug to be, taking into account the size of the tiles plus the width of the reducer strips—which Kristan is shown test-fitting **(B)**. Mark the corners of the overall measurements on the remnant, using a measuring tape and marking pen. Snap a chalk line to join the marks. Use a straightedge and a utility knife to make clean cuts along the marks. Use masking tape to tape off a ¾-inch-wide edge all the way around the edge of the rug backing to reserve a border space for the reducer strips.

2. Wearing rubber gloves apply water-base adhesive to the backing with a trowel **(C)**. Allow the adhesive to set according to the manufacturer's directions. Press the tiles into place, creating a pattern with different color tiles as desired **(D)**.

3. Remove the masking tape and secure the reducer strips **(E)**.

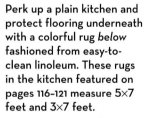

Perk up a plain kitchen and protect flooring underneath with a colorful rug *below* fashioned from easy-to-clean linoleum. These rugs in the kitchen featured on pages 116–121 measure 5×7 feet and 3×7 feet.

REFRESH A WOOD TABLE

If you have a stained-wood table that's seen better days, follow Dave Sheinkopf's lead and refresh the look with this technique from *Design on a Dime.*

STEP BY STEP

1. Sand the tabletop and wipe clean with a tack cloth. Use a 2-inch-wide paintbrush or foam brush to apply a liberal coat of Danish oil. Allow the Danish oil to set a few minutes, then wipe away the excess with a rag.
2. Following the manufacturer's directions for application suggestions and drying times, seal the tabletop by applying furniture wax with a rag **(A)**. As the wax dries, use an artist's brush and a rag to apply stain to touch up scratches on the table sides and base **(B)** and **(C)**.
3. Buff the waxed surface with a clean rag **(D)**.

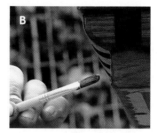

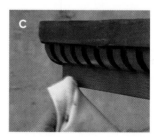

MATERIALS

Wood table

Danish oil that matches the original table finish

Furniture wax, clear or the desired shade*

Stain to match table

TOOLS

Fine-grit sandpaper

Tack cloth

2-inch-wide paintbrush or foam brush

Clean rags

Artist's brush

It's best to use colored wax on darker stained woods because clear wax, once it dries, sometimes shows against the dark wood.

To find a bargain-price secondhand table worthy of refreshing, shop thrift stores and flea markets. (This table is shown in the kitchen on pages 116–121.)

HOW TO INSTALL A SINK AND FAUCET

A fast and affordable way to freshen the look of your kitchen is to install a new sink and faucet. Tackle the job yourself with these easy-to-follow instructions.

MATERIALS

Sink

Faucet

Silicon sealant

Plumber's putty

Strainer set

TOOLS

Measuring tape

Flashlight

Basin wrench or crescent wrench

Water pump pliers

Bucket and towel

Long screwdriver

Putty knife

Jigsaw (if you need to enlarge the opening in the countertop)

Damp cloth

Make a trip to your neighborhood home center to scope out the plumbing aisle. You'll find sinks and faucets in several sizes, configurations, and finishes. Sinks typically come with a template you can lay on the countertop, trace, and cut out for a perfect fit.

STEP-BY-STEP SINK INSTALLATION

1. Measure the width of the base cabinet where the sink will be installed. Purchase a sink that is at least 4 inches narrower than the cabinet so you can install the sink without modifying the cabinetry. If your new sink is larger than your old one, you'll need to enlarge the countertop hole.

2. Follow the instructions in "Step-by-Step Faucet Installation" *opposite* to disconnect the faucet from the supply lines. Use a flashlight to see underneath the sink if needed. If you have a garbage disposal, turn off the breaker-panel switch that provides electricity to the kitchen and unplug the power cord on the disposal.

3. Disconnect the sink from the drainpipes using water pump pliers **(A)**. Keep a bucket and towel handy to clean up the water that inevitably will spill from the pipes. **Note:** *If you have a garbage disposal, continue to Step 4; if not, skip Step 4.*

4. Disconnect the disposal from the sink. Loosen the ring that attaches the disposal to the sink flange by inserting a long screwdriver into the lugs on the ring and twisting **(B)**. When the disposal is loose, lift it off the drainpipe. You also must remove the mounting bracket for the disposal from the bottom of the sink drain; you'll need to attach the disposal to the new sink. To remove the mounting bracket, pry the retaining clip off the drain flange **(C)**, then loosen the screws on the bracket.

5. Many sinks are secured to the countertop by clamps under the countertop. To remove the clamps, loosen their screws. Loosen the sink by inserting a putty knife under its edges. Lift out the sink; have a helper assist you.

6. The box containing the new sink should include a template that shows you how large the countertop opening must be. Use

it to check the existing opening. If your new sink is the same size as your old one, you should be able to drop it into the existing opening. If your new sink is larger, enlarge the opening by cutting it with a jigsaw, using the template as a guide. At this point if you plan to install a new faucet, install it now, following the instructions *right*.

7. Confirm the fit of the sink by setting it into the new hole, grasping the sink through the drain holes. Lift the sink out and apply silicon sealant around the edges of the opening, being sure not to leave any gaps. Set the sink in place. Press on the sink to set it in the sealant. If your sink requires clamps to secure it to the countertop, attach those now. Use a damp cloth to wipe excess sealant off the countertop. Let the sealant cure for 30 minutes.

8. Apply plumber's putty to the underside of each strainer flange and set the strainers into the holes **(D)**. On the underside of the sink, attach the gaskets that came with the strainers to the strainer flanges. Then attach the drainpipes to the strainers and tighten the nuts. **Note:** *You may need to adjust the lengths of the drainpipes if the shape of your new sink is different from*

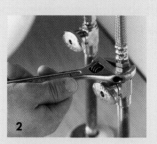

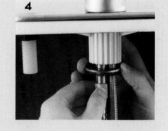

STEP-BY-STEP FAUCET INSTALLATION

1. The copper lines that supply hot and cold water to the sink often have shutoff valves under the sink. (Use a flashlight to see underneath the sink if needed.) Turn them off. **Note:** *You may need to turn off water elsewhere, such as at the lines in the basement that lead to the sink.* Turn the faucet on to let water and pressure drain from the lines.

2. Use a crescent wrench (or a basin wrench if the nuts are difficult to reach) to disconnect the faucet from the supply lines.

3. It's easiest to install a faucet on a new sink before the sink is put in place. Follow the installation instructions for your specific faucet. The process typically involves laying a gasket on the sink, then setting the faucet on top of the gasket with its tailpieces extending through the holes in the sink.

4. Tighten a nut on the underside of the sink to secure the faucet to the sink. Reconnect the faucet by reversing the steps you took to disconnect the water lines. Turn on the water to the kitchen.

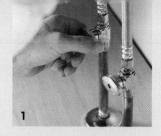

the old one. If you have a garbage disposal, reconnect it to the sink flange, insert its drainpipe, and plug in the power cord. Reconnect the faucet following the instructions in "Step-by-Step Faucet Installation" *above*.

9. For a few days after you finish the installation, watch the plumbing for leaks. If leaks occur tighten the fittings and add sealant or putty as needed.

HOW TO INSTALL LAMINATE FLOORING

A tongue-and-groove system that requires no glue makes installing many of today's laminate floors a snap. These steps show how to complete the job in a weekend.

MATERIALS

Laminate flooring

Underlayment (one roll covers approximately 100 square feet)

Laminate floor installation kit (available at home centers and specialty retailers)

Finishing nails (to reinstall trim pieces)

Shoe moldings (optional)

Transition strips (to connect the laminate floor to adjoining surfaces)

TOOLS

Pry bar

Measuring tape

Circular saw or handsaw

Jamb saw

Hammer and nail set (to reinstall trim pieces)

STEP BY STEP

1. The flooring should sit in the room for at least 48 hours prior to installation, allowing it to acclimate to the temperature and humidity. This prevents buckling and other problems after installation.
2. Pry the baseboard molding off the wall and set it aside for reinstallation at the end of the project. Remove old flooring, if necessary.
3. Clear the floor of staples or nails left from any flooring you tore out, then roll the underlayment out into the desired spaces **(A)** without overlapping the edges.
4. Decide which direction to lay the planks. Plan ahead so the last plank is at least

One of the conveniences of installing laminate flooring in a kitchen or dining room is that it can be installed directly over many other kinds of flooring, including old vinyl or tile. However you must remove carpeting or wood bonded to concrete.

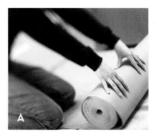

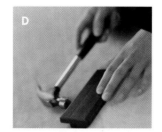

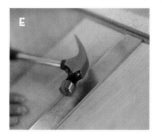

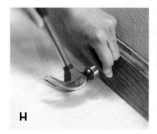

2 inches wide. If you measure across the room (figuring in a ¼-inch gap at each wall to allow the flooring to expand) and have a remainder that is less than 2 inches, add that value to the width of a full plank and divide by 2. This is the width of the first and last planks.

5. Depending on the results of your calculations from Step 4, you may have to rip (cut lengthwise) the first plank. When cutting laminate planks with a circular saw—whether ripping or cutting to length as shown—cut with the finished side down **(B)**. When using a handsaw, cut with the finished side up.

6. Install the first row of planks with the tongue side facing the wall. **Note:** *Some manufacturers recommend cutting the tongue edge off planks facing walls.* Join one plank to

another by connecting the tongues and grooves. You may be able to snugly connect the planks by hand, or you may need to use a pull bar from an installation kit to pull them tightly together **(C)**. Alternatively use a tapping block from an installation kit to tap the joints together **(D)**.

7. Always leave a ¼-inch gap between the planks and the wall **(E)** to allow the planks to expand. At the end of a row, cut the last plank to length **(F)**.

8. As you snap on new rows, allow at least 12 inches between the seams in adjoining rows. You often can start a new row with the scrap from the plank you cut at the end of the previous row, but use pieces shorter than 12 inches.

9. There should be only ¼ inch between the last row and the wall; in order to do this

you may need to slide the planks into position at an angle, then gently pry them into place with a pry bar.

10. Use a jamb saw to cut the door casing about 1⁄16 inch above the height of the laminate flooring, giving the planks room to slide under the casing. Achieve the proper height by using a piece of the flooring with underlayment at the casing as a spacer. Rest the jamb saw on the top and cut the casing to height **(G)**.

11. After all the laminate planks are in place, reinstall the baseboard moldings **(H)**. Install shoe moldings, if needed, over the expansion joints and use transition strips to connect the laminate floor to the adjoining surfaces. Laminate floors are designed to "float," so nails used to attach trim should never pass through the flooring.

TILE A BACKSPLASH

Surfacing the area between upper and lower cabinets with tile makes it easier to clean and adds a touch of style.

MATERIALS

Drywall or surfacing compound

Ceramic and/or tumbled-marble tile

Mastic

Grout

Grout sealer

Caulk

TOOLS

Level

Putty knife

Fine-grit sandpaper

Tack cloth

Measuring tape

Pencil, soft lead

Carpenter's level or framing square

Mastic trowel

Safety goggles

Work gloves

Scribing tool

Snap cutter

Rod saw or tile nippers

Tile spacers

Rubber-blade grout float

Rubber gloves

Tile sponge

Plastic bucket

Soft, dry cloth (or a cloth, plus a solution of water and white vinegar)

Small stiff-bristle brush

Masking tape

STEP BY STEP

1. To see how level the wall surface is, lay a level or long, straight board across the wall horizontally. Fill in low spots with a putty knife and drywall or surfacing compound; let dry. Sand the wall smooth and wipe with a tack cloth.

2. Use a measuring tape to locate the center of the wall. Using a level and pencil, draw horizontal and vertical guidelines **(A)**. Plot out your tile pattern and, starting at the midpoint, arrange a single row of tile in each direction to see how they fit. Adjust the spacing as needed to minimize cutting and waste. ***Note:*** *The best spacing may require straddling the center row of tile on the vertical or horizontal guideline, in which case your actual baseline will be slightly off-center. Be sure that tiled areas stop short of electrical boxes or extend beyond them; coverplates shouldn't overhang the outer row of tile. Using a level or a framing square, mark the final baselines.*

Interspersing another type of tile, such as more costly tumbled or hand-painted tiles, amid inexpensive field tiles is a good way to add interest and style while stretching the budget. Here tumbled pieces form a quilt-block design and are randomly distributed among field tiles on the backsplash.

3. Spread mastic on the wall with the smooth edge of the mastic trowel, then use the notched edge to cut a series of V-shape furrows **(B)**. Apply just enough mastic to set one or two short rows of tile at a time so you can adjust the spacing before the mastic hardens. Avoid covering your baselines with mastic until you're certain that the horizontal and vertical spacing is working out according to plan.

4. Before pressing a whole group of tiles into place, press on a single tile and then pry it off. Check the back side to see if the mastic is evenly distributed **(C)**. Voids or extra-thick deposits of mastic can weaken the bond. Repeat this test each time you apply a fresh swath of mastic. When you get to a tile that you need to cut, refer to "Cutting Tiles" *right*.

5. If your wall tile doesn't have built-in spacing lugs (nubs that protrude along the edges), add temporary spacers **(D)** to keep the tiles from shifting before the mastic hardens. ***Note:*** *Use spacers between the countertop and the first row of backsplash tile to leave room for caulking.*

6. Allow the tile to set at least 24 hours before grouting. For joints ⅛-inch or less, use unsanded grout; for larger joints, use sanded. Follow the package directions for mixing the grout, then apply immediately with a rubber-blade grout float **(E)**, holding the tool at an angle to help work the grout into the joints. Wear rubber gloves to protect your skin from irritants.

7. Wait about 10 minutes for the grout to firm up, then wipe off the excess with a tile sponge. Rinse the sponge in a pail of water after each pass. After the last sponging has dried, remove the final haze with a soft cloth or scrub it off with water or a solution of water and white vinegar. Dump the rinse water outdoors; grout deposits can clog waste lines.

8. Grout is porous and will stain easily if left unsealed. As soon as it has dried thoroughly (usually about three days), apply one or two coats of grout sealer with a small stiff-bristle brush. Use a soft, dry cloth to remove excess sealer from the tile itself as you work; some sealers can discolor tile finishes. Where the tile meets the countertop, run a double strip of masking tape along the joint, then fill the joint with caulk and smooth it with a wet finger. When the caulk dries, peel off the tape.

CUTTING TILES

FOLLOW THESE INSTRUCTIONS to cut tiles. When cutting tile, wear safety goggles and work gloves.

LAY THE TILE FACE UP, directly on top of the whole tile it will adjoin. Butt another whole tile against the edge you're cutting to and overlap the tile to be cut. Scribe the face of the first tile along the edge of the lapped one, etching through the glaze; this helps minimize chipping when you cut the tile.

FOR STRAIGHT CUTS lay the tile face up on the bed of a snap cutter *above*. Position your scored mark under the scoring wheel of the cutter and lock the tile into place with the adjustable brace. Apply firm steady pressure as you draw the scoring wheel across the tile. After scoring park the wheel in the slot above the tile and exert firm downward pressure on the lever arm. The tile should snap neatly apart along the scored line. A few tiles will break no matter how careful you are, so expect to redo some cuts.

FOR IRREGULAR CUTS use either a rod saw or a pair of tile nippers. Before using either tool, practice on a piece of scrap tile to get a feel for the technique, then proceed cautiously.

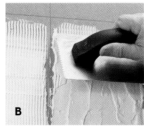
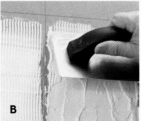

PLANNING GUIDE
AND **ARRANGING** KIT

Now that your thought processes are primed with functional designs and ideas to make your kitchen stylish, you're ready to plan. In this section you'll evaluate your current kitchen and consider future needs. You'll also find advice for selecting the professionals you'll need, such as a designer or contractor. As you work on the budget, the handy cost chart can help you estimate prices for the components you want. Wrapping up this section is a useful arranging kit with templates and graph paper so you can experiment with kitchen layouts to your heart's content.

KITCHEN COMPONENT ANALYSIS

Whether your kitchen is in need of a decorative facelift or a major overhaul, these tips can help you invest your dollars wisely.

Before beginning your kitchen makeover, analyze your present kitchen, listing what you like and dislike about it. This will help you determine if your renovation will be primarily cosmetic, structural, or a combination of both. Changing flooring, cabinets, and countertops may solve a style issue, but adding storage space or reworking traffic flow may require more costly remodeling.

FUTURE PLANS Assess your personal situation, including how you will use your kitchen now and in coming years. If you plan to live in your house for 10 or more years and you cook or entertain frequently, greater remodeling expenses are justified than if you will be moving within a few years and you rarely eat at home. Although an updated kitchen makes a good selling point, keep the overall value of your home in mind if you want to recoup renovation costs soon.

NITTY-GRITTY DETAILS Before making any purchases, take accurate measurements of your kitchen and then visit model displays to determine the features and components you want. If you will be expanding your space, consider how much more room you will need

for the amenities you desire. As you shop different retailers, ask for price quotes. Be certain that the dollar amount each retailer supplies is an equal comparison in terms of size and quality of appliances, fixtures, and cabinets. Clarify delivery and installation charges, warranties, and service options. (You'll also find additional kitchen component costs in the chart beginning on page 179.) Whether your budget is large or small, make quality a priority: Leaky faucets, sagging doors, and sticking drawers are irritating and may be difficult, if not impossible, to repair.

THE BOTTOM LINE Getting price quotes for all the products you want accounts for the "hard costs" of your kitchen makeover, but these numbers don't tell the complete story. These costs may equal less than half the total cost of a project once you add labor and unseen material costs including flooring underlayments, plumbing updates, and additional electrical lines.

Just how much of your budget goes to labor depends on the scope of the project and the region where you live. In a simple tear-out-and-replace job in the heartland, labor may total only one-third of the costs. On the

coasts labor costs may double that amount. If there are major structural changes—moving and removing walls, windows, and doors—the percentage will also be greater. Plus certain kinds of cabinets and surfaces are more difficult to install than others, which affects labor costs. The bottom line: Ask questions before settling on any particular component; a look-alike may be more cost effective.

Most kitchen designers agree that cabinetry is the biggest variable in the budget and the easiest place to save or splurge. The key to gauging cabinetry costs is counting "boxes." A box is an individual cabinet unit, such as a base cabinet, a wall cabinet, or a set of drawers. Per-box averages (often listed in manufacturer literature as the average cost of a 24-inch base cabinet) may cost anywhere from $200 for stock cabinets to $2,000 for custom models. The more boxes you use, the higher the cabinetry cost.

If, after adding up all the variables, a new kitchen seems too costly, consider making only cosmetic changes now and wait a few years before undertaking a major renovation. As technology advances and styles evolve, requirements for that "perfect kitchen" will continue to keep you wanting more.

PRIORITY CHECKLIST

Planning the kitchen you want requires understanding the kitchen you have. Then you need to think about what you'd like to change and how you'd change it.

This quiz will help you identify what kind of kitchen you're living with now, what its advantages and drawbacks are, what your needs are, and what you'd like to have in your new kitchen.

First evaluate your current kitchen using this list of questions. Use the box beside each question to indicate how important it is to rectify any problems you identify. Follow this number system or devise your own: 1 = must fix, 2 = want to fix, 3 = would be nice to fix, but can live with it the way it is.

Consider how the higher-priority problems may be rectified in a renovation or avoided altogether if you're building a new kitchen.

With your prioritized kitchen uses in mind, also note what storage needs, work centers, and appliances your new or remodeled kitchen will have.

Refer to this questionnaire as you continue to plan your kitchen and take it with you when you talk to your kitchen designer, architect, or contractor.

For more information on **designing your own kitchen,** visit *HGTV.com/kitchenplanner*

KITCHEN QUIZ

Use this list of questions to identify the features of your current kitchen that you want to change when you build or remodel. Use each box to note the priority: 1 = high priority, 2 = medium priority, 3 = low priority.

STORAGE
☐ Are your cabinets crowded?

☐ Could you relocate a passageway and reclaim space for cabinetry?

☐ Would you like a walk-in pantry or a pantry cabinet?

☐ Are your existing refrigerator and freezer large enough?

COOKING
☐ Are you cut off from others when preparing meals?

☐ Are there workstations for multiple cooks?

☐ Are there too many steps between appliances and the sink?

☐ Is there ample counter space beside the cooktop and refrigerator?

☐ Does your kitchen meet the needs of your special cooking interests?

CLEANUP
☐ Is the dishwasher near the sink?

☐ Should the table be closer to the sink and dishwasher?

☐ Could you benefit from a second dishwasher?

☐ Is there a place for recyclables?

SURFACES
☐ Are you pleased with the current surfaces?

☐ Are the surfaces easy to clean?

☐ Is the flooring comfortable?

LIGHT AND VIEWS
☐ Is your kitchen shadowy?

☐ Do you have pleasant views from the sink and the range?

DINING
☐ Do you have a place for dining in the kitchen?

☐ Do you encounter seating difficulties when you entertain?

TRAFFIC
☐ Do entries impede the work core?

☐ Does the table block entries?

☐ Does traffic interrupt cooking?

☐ Are other traffic problems apparent?

CHOOSE THE PROS
AND SURVIVE THE MESS

Whether you're searching for an architect, an interior designer, or a remodeling contractor, use these tactics to track down the best professionals to design and execute your kitchen decorating or remodeling project. Then follow the survival tips to make the best of the mess.

GATHER
Collect the names of professionals to investigate and interview. Ask friends and colleagues for suggestions and recommendations. Identify local referrals with the help of professional organizations, such as the American Institute of Architects (AIA), 800/242-3837, website: aia.org; the National Association of Home Builders Remodelers Council (NAHB), 800/368-5242 ext. 8216, website: nahb.com; the National Association of the Remodeling Industry (NARI), 800/611-6274, website: nari.org; or the American Society of Interior Designers (ASID), 202/546-3480, website: asid.org. These websites can help you find a contractor in your area: handymanonline.com; improvenet.com; remodelnet.com; and homeownersreferral.com.

EXPLORE
Call the professionals on your list—you should have four or five from each profession—and ask for references. Contact the clients they name and ask them to recount their positive and negative experiences. Also if you've seen a recent decorating or remodeling project that you like, contact the homeowners and ask about their experience and results.

EVALUATE
Based on these references, interview your top three choices and tour some of their finished projects. Savvy architects and contractors will ask you questions as well to determine your expectations and needs. You should come away from each interview and tour with an idea of the quality of their work and how well your personalities and visions for the project match.

SOLICIT
To narrow your choices, it may be worth the additional cost to solicit preliminary drawings from each professional. This is a great way to test your working relationship and to gather options from which to choose. Also ask contractors for bids. Don't base your decision on cost alone, but weigh what you learned in the interview with the thoroughness of the bid itself.

SIGN UP
Before beginning a project with any professional, have the facts on paper to legally protect you before, during, and after the work is done. Define the scope of the project and fees as specifically as possible. The contract should include a clear description of the work to be done, materials that will be required, and who will supply them. It should also spell out commencement and completion dates, any provisions relating to timeliness, and your total costs (subject to additions and deductions by a written change order only). Payments should be tied to work stages; be wary of any contractor who wants a lot of money up front. If ordering certain materials needs to be done weeks in advance (to allow time for manufacturing), get a list of all those materials and their cost before committing to up-front money. Kitchens, for example, may require a sizable cash advance to finance appliances and cabinetry. If possible, make out these initial checks to the subcontractors and retailers directly.

SURVIVAL TIPS
When your home transforms into a construction zone, the mess can make you wonder if your life will ever be back to normal. To ensure the minor inconveniences of a decorating makeover or a remodeling project don't become major headaches, discuss cleanup with your contractor before work begins. Have a team meeting with all the key professionals and ask for an overview of the entire project so together you can develop a plan to minimize disruption.

Ask workers to arrive and leave at reasonable hours. Noise is inevitable. Understand that if you set shorter workdays, you will also be setting, and possibly lengthening, the duration of the project. Let the contractor know in advance if there are any holidays or special family events when your house will be off-limits.

Set up "temporary rooms." When remodeling the kitchen, move the refrigerator, the coffee pot, and the microwave to the dining room. If you don't want workers to use your restrooms, set up a portable toilet near the entrance to the remodeling area.

Be flexible. No matter how meticulously you schedule your project, there is bound to be a surprise or two. Go with the flow and be willing to change a discontinued fabric, tile, or fixture.

Start calculating your kitchen costs with our alphabetical product listing. Except where noted, prices do not include labor and installation.

ITEM	DESCRIPTION	COST
CABINETRY	**READY-MADE** limited choices in sizes, woods, finishes, and door styles; quality varies depending on cabinetry line	$100–$200 per linear foot w/o hardware
	SEMICUSTOM wide range of sizes, woods, finishes, and door styles; good quality	$125–$650 per linear foot w/o hardware
	CUSTOM any size, shape, and finish; exotic woods available; high attention to detail	$500–$1,000 per linear foot w/o hardware
COOKTOP	**BASIC FOUR-BURNER** 30- to 36-inch electric coil or gas; porcelain or stainless steel; better gas models have sealed burners	$250–$450
	ELECTRIC SMOOTHTOP OR GAS UNIT with glass/ceramic top and sealed burners; top models have designer looks, five burners	$450–$1,200
	PROFESSIONAL-GRADE GAS UNIT with five or six burners (sealed or unsealed), higher Btus for faster heating	$1,300–$4,800
MICROWAVE	**SMALL COUNTERTOP MODEL** 600–800 watts, up to 1 cubic foot; better models include turntables and auto-sensor cooking	$70–$325
	FULL-SIZE COUNTERTOP MODEL 1.3–2.2 cubic feet, 1,100+ watts; priciest: convection	$170–$450+
	OVER-THE-RANGE microwave-hood combination	$300–$1,600
	BUILT-IN MICROWAVE-CONVECTION OVEN $300+ without convection	$600–$1,500
RANGE	**BASIC 30-INCH MODEL** with electric coils or gas burners (some sealed); not self-cleaning	$300–$550
	ELECTRIC SMOOTHTOP priciest models feature stainless steel, slide-in styling, convection or double oven	$500–$2,000
	DUAL FUEL any finish; professional-grade	$1,000–$9,000+
	30-INCH GAS stainless steel, burners up to 12,000 Btus* (sealed available)	$1,000–$2,700
	PROFESSIONAL-GRADE GAS 36- to 60-inch, 15,000+ Btus, double oven and/or dual fuel	$3,800–$9,000+
WALL OVENS	**BASIC ELECTRIC OR GAS OVEN** up to 27 inches	$400–$900
	SINGLE OVEN WITH CONVECTION FEATURES double oven up to 30 inches	$750–$1,900
	DOUBLE OVEN WITH CONVECTION FEATURES or combination unit (microwave oven over oven)	$1,400–$3,200
	PROFESSIONAL-GRADE DOUBLE OVEN stainless steel or designer color	$2,800–$5,000+

*Btus are British Thermal Units—a measurement of energy. The higher the Btus that an appliance offers, the more cooking power it delivers.

ITEM	DESCRIPTION	COST
COUNTERTOPS	**CERAMIC TILE** basic, but glass or art tiles are significantly higher; per sq. ft.	$2–$10
	BUTCHER BLOCK per sq. ft.	$20–$80
	LAMINATE installed, per linear ft.	$30–$40
	QUARTZ installed, per sq. ft.	$35–$115
	SOLID SURFACING installed, per sq. ft.	$45–$85
	STONE OR CONCRETE installed, per sq. ft.	$60–$100+
DISHWASHER	**BASIC MODEL** plastic or enameled-steel interior, some touchpads	$300–$525
	QUIET more cycles and convenience features, built-in garbage disposal, stainless steel available	$600–$850
	ULTRAQUIET designer looks or stainless-steel exteriors, better tub, feature-laden	$900–$1,700
	OTHER OPTIONS dishwasher drawer (single unit, $700; double unit, $1,400), 30-inch-wide dishwasher ($2,500)	$700–$2,500
FAUCET	**BASIC** chrome or colored epoxy, one or two handles, standard or high-arc spout; better models have solid-brass construction	$60–$180
	PULLOUT	$150–$600
	CHROME AND OTHER OPTIONS stylish, higher quality finishes	$200–$1,000
POT-FILLER	**BASIC WALL-MOUNT** with extendable spout that swivels and folds up against the wall	$200–$750
	COMMERCIAL-STYLE with pull-down sprayer	$650–$1,000
FLOORING	**VINYL SHEET**	$6–$39 per sq. yd.
	VINYL TILE	$1–$6 per sq. ft.
	CERAMIC TILE art tile significantly higher	$2–$7 per tile
	LINOLEUM	$3–$6 per sq. ft.
	CORK	$4–$11 per sq. ft.
	LAMINATE priciest: tile look	$4–$13 per sq. ft.
	SLATE, GRANITE, OR LIMESTONE	$5–$30 per sq. ft.
	MARBLE OR TRAVERTINE	$5–$30 per sq. ft.
	HARDWOOD solid or engineered	$8–$30 per sq. ft.
GARBAGE DISPOSAL	**1/3–5/8 HORSEPOWER** continuous feed, low-duty	$60–$100
	UP TO 1 HP quiet, heavy-duty, some with auto-reverse or anti-jam features	$150–$250
	PROFESSIONAL-GRADE all stainless steel, auto-reverse, anti-jam features	$500+

ITEM	DESCRIPTION	COST
REFRIGERATOR-FREEZER	**BASIC TOP- OR BOTTOM-MOUNT** 17.6–22 cubic feet, icemaker option	$550–$750
	BETTER TOP- OR BOTTOM-MOUNT with more convenience features	$800–$2,600
	SIDE-BY-SIDE counter-depth model for built-in look at high end	$800–$3,000
	FULL-SIZE BUILT-IN commercial-grade or luxury model; Internet/computer available	$3,000–$8,000
	INTEGRATED BELOW-COUNTER REFRIGERATOR OR FREEZER DRAWERS	$2,700
SINK	**ENAMELED STEEL OR BASIC ACRYLIC** thin (20+ gauge) stainless steel, no soundproofing	$60–$200
	ENAMELED CAST IRON two bowls (add about $75 for a polished brass drain/strainer)	$150–$600
	SOLID SURFACING	$250–$1,000
	BETTER STAINLESS STEEL 18 gauge with soundproofing, satin finish, deeper bowls	$350–$1,000
	APRON-FRONT high-end; copper, stone	$800–$2,000+
	GOURMET WORK SINK three-bowl with drainboard	$1,500–$4,000+
TRASH COMPACTOR	**BASIC WHITE OR BLACK** controls on console	$400–$525
	STAINLESS-STEEL EXTERIOR	$525–$800
	PROFESSIONAL-GRADE stainless steel, integrated style (cabinet-panel ready)	$750–$1,400+
VENTILATION HOOD	**STANDARD** wall-mount hood, filter or exhaust, 180–350 cubic feet per minute (cfm)*	$75–$400
	BETTER-QUALITY updraft/downdraft, including stainless-steel canopies; up to 600 cfm	$550–$1,000+
	HIGH-PERFORMANCE stainless steel, chimney-style or wall canopy	$1,000–$2,000+
	SEMICUSTOM OR CUSTOM DESIGN high-end glass-and-steel combination	$1,700–$5,000+
WARMING DRAWER	**24- TO 27-INCH** black, white, or stainless steel	$600–$850
	30-INCH stainless-steel or custom panels, more options	$750–$1,350
WINE COOLER	**BASIC** 25–50 bottle capacity, one adjustable temperature	$270–$900
	PROFESSIONAL-GRADE with multiple temperature zones; high-end: double capacity	$1,200–$5,000

*Ventilation hoods are rated by cubic feet per minute, or cfm, which is the amount of air that the appliance draws. The higher the cfm rating, the more efficient the hood. Buy the highest rating you can afford.

ARRANGING KIT

Here is everything you need—templates of common kitchen components and grid paper—to experiment with floor plan arrangements for your new kitchen.

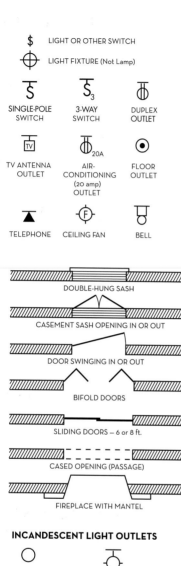

Even if you plan to work with a professional designer, you'll find it beneficial to "test drive" some potential layout ideas for your kitchen. Share these preliminary plans with your designer to best communicate your needs and the floor plan arrangements that make you feel most comfortable.

Photocopy the grid paper on page 187 and plot out the dimensions of your planned kitchen space. If you're remodeling within an existing kitchen space, take careful measurements—including the locations of doors and windows—and transfer those to the grid paper. (One square equals 1 square foot of floor space.) Use the architectural symbols to mark the position of existing architectural features. If you plan to add some of these features, use a different color to indicate what is new, such as built-ins or new fixtures. Use dotted lines to mark obstructions, including prominent light fixtures and angled

ceilings. If you're building a new addition, mark the existing structure in one color and use a different color to mark the addition. Whether your kitchen will be remodeled, part of an addition, or located in a new house, plot the space as well as its relationship to adjacent areas, including any mudroom, hall, pantry, and sitting or snacking areas.

Then photocopy and cut out the templates on the following pages and arrange and rearrange the components on your grid paper plan. If you own an existing piece of furniture that you want to include in your kitchen plan, such as a table or freestanding island, measure the piece, draw it to scale (1 square on the grid paper equals 1 square foot of space), and cut out the new template to use on the grid plan. Once you find one or two arrangements that you like best, trace the templates directly onto the grid paper.

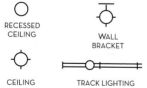

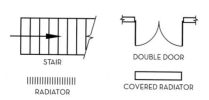

WALL CABINETS

Standard Cabinet Heights: 12, 15, 18, 24, 27, 30, 36, 42, and 48 inches.

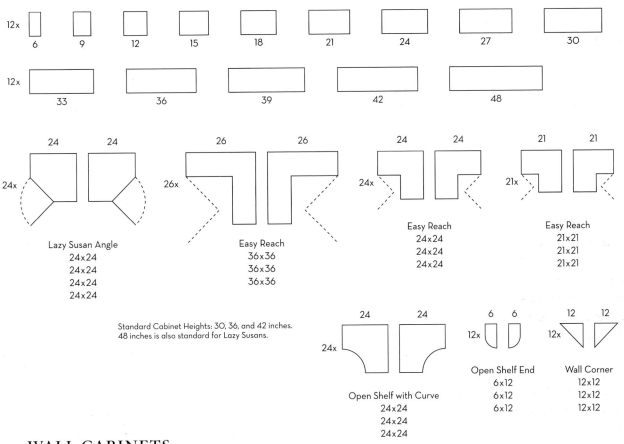

Standard Cabinet Heights: 30, 36, and 42 inches.
48 inches is also standard for Lazy Susans.

WALL CABINETS —
PENINSULA WALL PIECES

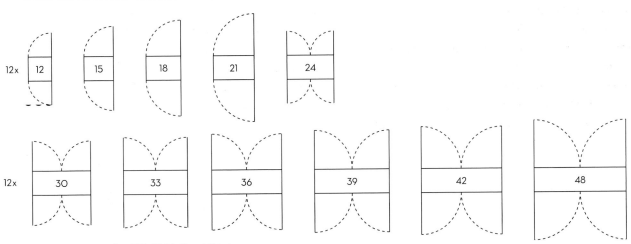

Standard Cabinet Heights: 23½, 30, 36, 42, and 48 inches.

WALL CABINETS — STORAGE ANGLES (APPLIANCE GARAGE)

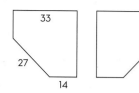

Standard Cabinet Height: 18 1/2 inches.

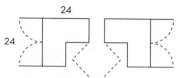

Wall Easy Reach
24x24
24x24
24x24

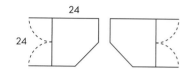

Wall Angle
24x24
24x24
24x24

Standard Cabinet Heights: 30, 36, and 42 inches.

BASE CABINETS

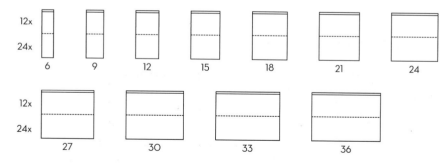

| 6 | 9 | 12 | 15 | 18 | 21 | 24 |

27   30   33   36

Standard Cabinet Heights: 34 1/2 inches.

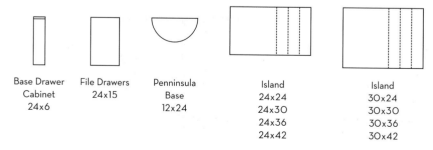

Base Drawer
Cabinet
24x6

File Drawers
24x15

Penninsula
Base
12x24

Island
24x24
24x30
24x36
24x42

Island
30x24
30x30
30x36
30x42

Standard Cabinet Height: 34 1/2 inches. Standard File Drawer Height: 28 1/2 inches.

BASE CABINETS — BLIND BASE CORNER

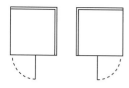

Blind Base Corner
24x24

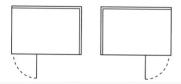

Blind Base Corner
36x24

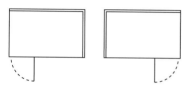

Blind Base Corner
39x24

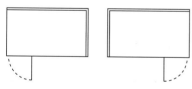

Blind Base Corner
42x24

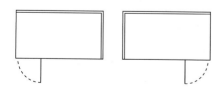

Blind Base Corner
45x24

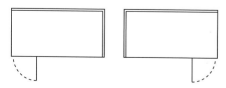

Blind Base Corner
48x24

Standard Cabinet Height: 34 1/2 inches.

OPEN
SHELF
FOR
BASE END

36x24

39x24

42x24

45x24

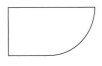

48x24

Standard Cabinet Height: 34½ inches.

SINK BASES (SINK DEPTHS VARY)

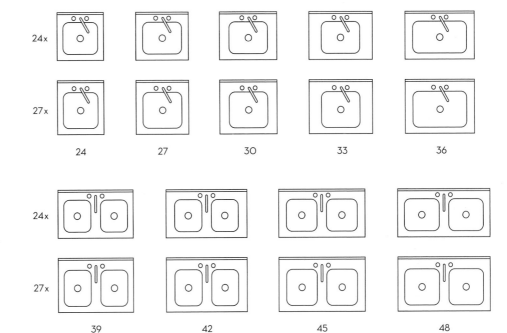

24x

27x

24   27   30   33   36

24x

27x

39   42   45   48

BASE CORNER CABINETS

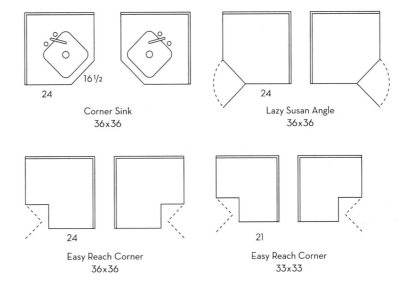

24 16½

Corner Sink
36x36

24

Lazy Susan Angle
36x36

24

Easy Reach Corner
36x36

21

Easy Reach Corner
33x33

Standard Cabinet Height: 34½ inches.

PANTRIES

12x
24x

9   12

12x
24x

15   18

12x
24x

24

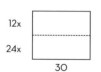

12x
24x

30

Standard Cabinet Heights:
84, 90, and 96 inches.

COOKTOPS

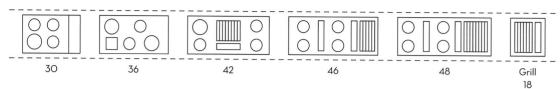

30   36   42   46   48   Grill
18

DROP-IN RANGES

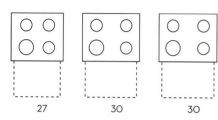

27   30   30

FREESTANDING RANGES

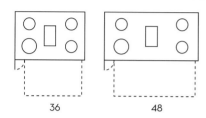

36   48

MICROWAVE OVENS

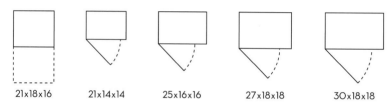

21x18x16   21x14x14   25x16x16   27x18x18   30x18x18

WALL OVENS

Wall Oven
27x24x81

Double
Wall Oven
30x24x81

Double
Wall Oven
33x24x81

Warming
Drawer
30x24x34 1/2

REFRIGERATORS

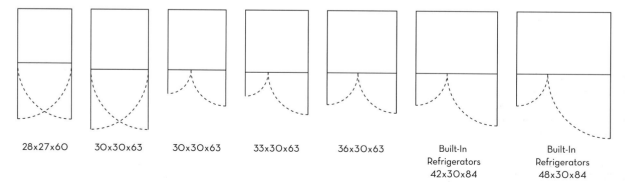

28x27x60   30x30x63   30x30x63   33x30x63   36x30x63   Built-In
Refrigerators
42x30x84

Built-In
Refrigerators
48x30x84

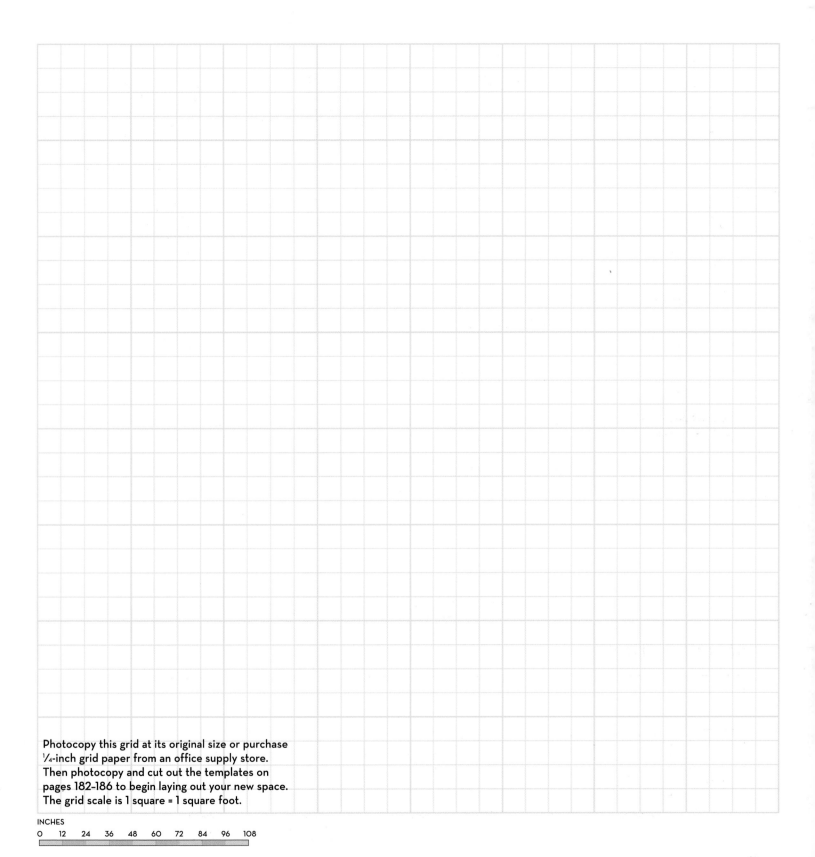

Photocopy this grid at its original size or purchase ¼-inch grid paper from an office supply store. Then photocopy and cut out the templates on pages 182–186 to begin laying out your new space. The grid scale is 1 square = 1 square foot.

INCHES

0   12   24   36   48   60   72   84   96   108

To see more rooms designed by many of the professionals listed below, visit HGTV.com/designers

PAGES 12-17, HEART OF THE HOME
Photographer. Cameron Sadeghpour
Designer/Builder. Haskins Design Group, Residential Designers and Master Builders, P.O. Box 57, 101 Main St., Booneville, IA 50038; 515/987-2277; fax: 515/987-2278; e-mail: haskinsdesigngroup@mchsi.com
Resources. *Cabinetmaker:* Medallion Cabinetry; 952/442-5171; website: medallioncabinetry.com. *Appliances:* KitchenAid; 800/422-1230; website: kitchenaid.com. *Bamboo flooring:* Phillips Floors; 515/961-7300. *Countertops:* Midwest Tile, Marble, and Granite, Inc.; 515/334-0139

PAGES 20-23, MINI-BENEFITS
Photographer. Cameron Sadeghpour
Designer. Andrea Lainson, Regency Builders; 515/270-1497
Builder. Regency Builders; 515/270-1497; website: showplacekitchens.com
Resources. *Cabinets:* Showplace Kitchens; 515/251-4800; website: showplacekitchens.com. *Countertops:* Quality Marble & Tile; 515/289-0202. *Refrigerator:* Maytag; 800/688-9900; website: maytag.com

PAGES 26-29, STREAMLINED COOKING; *Kitchen Trends 2005, episode 101*
Photographer. John Ellis
Designer. Chris Tosdevin, 153 South Robertson Blvd., Los Angeles, CA 90048; 800/285-8428
Resources. *Cabinets:* Bulthaup; website: bulthaup.com. *Cooktop and ovens:* Gaggenau, 800/828-9165; website: gaggenau-usa.com. *Refrigerator and refrigerated drawer:* Sub-Zero Freezer Co. Inc; 800/222-7820; website: subzero.com

PAGES 32-35, WINE CELLAR SAVOIR FAIRE
Photographer. Cameron Sadeghpour
Builder. Tyler Homes, P.O. Box 413, Altoona, IA 50009; 515/957-9017; website: Tylerhomesiowa.com.
Resources. *Cabinetry:* Mid Continent Cabinetry; 651/234-3500; website: midcontinentcabinetry.com. *Countertop:* Bertini Marble and Tile; 515/222-9600; website: topgranite.com. *Cultured stone:* Glen-Gery Brick; 610/374-4011; website: glengerybrick.com. *Tile floor:* Flooring Gallery; website: flooring-gallery.com. *Wine:* The Wine Experience; 515/252-8798

PAGES 38-45, EASY ENTERTAINING
Photographer. Cameron Sadeghpour
Designer. Cheri Hausner, Ames Kitchen Design, 2006 E. Lincoln Way, Ames, IA; 515/232-7155
Resources. *Cabinets:* Crystal Cabinet Works Inc.; 800/347-5046; website: crystalcabinets.com. *Sinks and Faucets:* Kohler Company; 800/456-4537; website: kohler.com. *Dishwasher drawer:* Fisher & Paykel Appliances, Inc.; 800/863-5394; website: fisherpaykel.com. *Accessories:* Bed, Bath, and Beyond; 800/462-3966; website: bedbathandbeyond.com

PAGES 48-53, CABINET CAMPAIGN
Photographer. Andy Lyons
Designer. Cathy Kramer, Cathy Kramer Designs
Resources. *Microwave and range:* Amana; 800/843-0304; website: amana.com. *Flooring:* Pergo; 800/337-3746; website: pergo.com. *Hardware:* Liberty Hardware; 800/542-3789; website: libertyhardware.com. *Countertop (Kala Hari):* Silestone by Consentino; 866/430-3455; website: silestone.com. *Blue pendant light fixtures:* Tiella; 847/410-4400; website: tiella.com. *Baskets, bar stools, seat cushions, table, chairs:* Pier 1 Imports; 800/447-4371; website: pier1.com. *Paint (walls—SW6107 Nomadic Desert; upper cabinets—SW6105 Divine White; lower cabinets—SW6523 Denim):* Sherwin Williams; website: sherwin-williams.com. *Magnetic paint:* Kling Magnetic Paint; 518/392-4000; website: kling.com. *Backsplash tile:* Dal-Tile; 214/398-1411; website: daltile.com. *Sink and faucet:* Moen; 800/289-6636; website: moen.com. *Storage containers, pantry shelves and drawers:* Container Store; 888/266-8246; website: containerstore.com. *Wooden brackets:* Lowe's; 800/890-5932; website: lowes.com. *Dishes:* World Market; website: costplus.com. *Windows:* Windsor Windows; website: windsorwindows.com.

PAGES 56-59, ACCENT ON ACCESS
Photographer. Hopkins Associates
Designer. Chris Berry, ASID, NCIDQ certified; Brooksberry Kitchens & Baths; 751 Old Frontenac Sq., St. Louis, MO 63131; 314/872-7720
Builder. Stephen Ellerbrake, Ellerbrake Construction, 1309 Scott Troy Rd., Lebanon, IL 62254; 618/632-7745
Resources. *Range:* Viking Range Corp.; 888/845-4641; website: vikingrange.com. *Exhaust fan:* Best by Broan; 800/558-1711; website: broan.com. *Refrigerator:* Sub-Zero Freezer Co., Inc.; 800/222-7820; website: subzero.com. *Dishwasher:* Bosch; 800/866-2022; website: boschappliances.com. *Microwave:* KitchenAid; 800/422-1230; website: kitchenaid.com. *Cabinetry and hardware:* Rutt Custom Cabinetry, LLC; 800/420-7888; website: rutt1.com. *Countertops:* Shivakachi granite fabricated by Brooksberry Kitchens & Baths; 314/872-7720. *Flooring:* Bruce Hardwood Floors, a division of Triangle Pacific Corp., 800/722-4647; website: bruce.com. *Sinks:* Kindred Industries; 705/526-5427; website: kindred-sinkware.com

PAGES 62-67, HIDDEN ASSETS; *Designers' Challenge, episode 704*
Photographer. Edmund Barr
Designers. Judy Svendsen, ASID, DLF, CID; Raven Interiors; 626/798-6261. Mary Fisher Knott, Mary Fisher Designs, P.O. Box 14393, Scottsdale, AZ 85267; 480/473-0986; website: maryfisherdesigns.com
Resources. *Cabinetmaker:* CCA Woodworking; 626/303-6068. *Refrigerator:* Sub-Zero Freezer Co. Inc.; 800/222-7802; website: subzero.com. *Range:* Wolf Appliance Company; 800/332-9513; website: wolfappliance.com. *Sinks and faucets:* Franke Consumer Products Inc., Kitchen Systems Division; 800/626-5771; website: frankeksd.com. *Door handles:* Those Gringos; 480/905-3000. *Cabinet hardware:* Service Supply Co.; 626/795-2909; website: servicesupplyco.com. *Stone and tile:* Southland Stone; 800/778-2730. Century Granite & Marble Inc.; 818/767-8453. *Light fixtures:* Pasadena Lighting; 626/564-1112. *Flooring:* Superior Hardwood Flooring; 818/376-1415. *Lighting:* F.I.R.E., L.T.D.; 310/652-9110

PAGES 70-73, A COOK'S KITCHEN; *Designers' Challenge, episode 901*
Photographer. Ken Gutmaker
Designer. Maloos Anvarian, ASID, CID, Design with Maloos, 550 15th St. Suite M-10, San Francisco, CA 94103; 415/864-3857; website: maloos@designwithmaloos.com
Resources. *Salvaged architectural items:* Ohmega Salvage; 510/843-7368; website: ohmegasalvage.com

PAGES 78-83, TIMELESS CONTEMPORARY
Photographer. Cameron Sadeghpour
Architect/Builder. Phillip Vlieger, associate AIA, PineApple Homes, 219½ Fifth St., West Des Moines, IA 50265; 515/271-8175; website: pineapplehomes.net
Resources. *Accessories:* Abante Furnishings; 515/278-8621. *Dishwasher, range, microwave oven:* Bosch; 800/944-2904; website: boschappliances.com. *Refrigerator:* Frigidaire; website: frigidaire.com. *Cabinetmaker:* Consolidated Kitchens and Fireplaces; 800/888-2667; website: consolidatedkitchens.com. *Countertops:* A.J. Frank Inc.; 515/727-0613. *Flooring:* Phillips Floors; 515/961-7300. *Lighting:* Alpha Sound & Lighting; 800/523-8195; website: alphasoundandlighting.com

PAGES 86–91, ARTFUL ACCESSORIZING
Photographer. Andy Lyons
Builder. Wilmore Custom Homes, 8120 Heatherbow, Johnston, IA 50131; 515/249-3999
Resources. *Cabinetry layout:* Sunderland Brothers, Urbandale, IA 50322; 800/366-3226; *Cabinetry:* Merillat Industries Inc.; 800/575-8763; website: merillat.com. *Countertop:* Bertini Marble; 515/222-9600. *Tile:* Florida Tile; 800/789-8453; website: floridatile.com. *Accessories:* Bed, Bath, and Beyond; 800/462-3966; website: bedbathandbeyond.com. Pier 1 Imports; 800/447-4371; website: pier1.com

PAGES 94–97, HIDE AND SEEK
Photographer. Andy Lyons
Designer. Cathy Kramer, Cathy Kramer Designs
Resources. *Paint:* Glidden; 800/454-3336; glidden.com. *Pendant light fixture:* Kichler; 800/875-4216; website: .kichler.com. *Hardware:* Amerock; 800/435-6959; website: amerock.com. *Backsplash tile:* Dal-Tile; 214/398-1411; website: daltile.com. *Wood blinds:* Hunter Douglas; 800/265-1363; website: hunterdouglas.com. *Sink and faucet:* Moen; 800/289-6636; moen.com. *Countertop:* Silestone by Consentino; 866/430-3455; website: silestone.com

PAGE 100–105, FAMILY ALLURE
Photographer. Cameron Sadeghpour
Builder. Tyler Homes, P.O. Box 413, Altoona, IA 50009; 515/957-9017; website: Tylerhomesiowa.com
Resources. *Cabinetry:* Mid Continent Cabinetry; 651/234-3500; website: midcontinentcabinetry.com. *Countertops:* Bertini Marble and Tile; 515/222-9600; website: topgranite.com. *Home appliances:* KitchenAid; 800/422-1230; website: kitchenaid.com. *Architectural elements:* Enkeboll Design; 800/745-5507; website: enkeboll.com. *Tile floor:* Flooring Gallery; website: flooring-gallery.com

PAGES 108–113, TRUE COLORS
Photographer. Andy Lyons
Designer. Cathy Kramer, Cathy Kramer Designs
Resources. *Decorative knobs and hand-painted murals on cabinetry:* Sticks, Inc.; 515/246-8572; website: sticks.com

PAGES 116–119, FASHION FORWARD; *Design on a Dime,* episode 707
Photographer. Michael Garland
Designers. *Design on a Dime* designer Kristan Cunningham, design coordinator Spencer Anderson, and design coordinator Dave Sheinkopf; Home and Garden Television; website: HGTV.com
Resources. *Decorative project materials:* Lowe's Companies Inc.; 800/445-6937; website: lowes.com. Target Department Store; 800/800-8800; website: target.com. Home Goods; 661/253-0477. *Furniture:* Al's Discount Furniture; 818/255-4740. Rose Bowl Flea Market; 626/577-3100; website: rgcshows.com. *Flooring:* Linoleum City; 800/559-2489; website: linoleumcity.com. *Paint:* Behr Process Corp. (Behr paint is available at Home Depot); 800/854-0133, ext. 2; website: behr.com

PAGES 122–125, PERSONAL REFLECTIONS; *Design on a Dime,* episode 810
Photographer. Michael Garland
Designers. *Design on a Dime* designer Kristan Cunningham, design coordinator Spencer Anderson, and design coordinator Dave Sheinkopf; Home and Garden Television; website: HGTV.com
Resources. *Decorative project materials:* IKEA North America; 800/434-4532; ikea.com. Target Department Store; 800/800-8800; website: target.com. Cost Plus World Market; 310/441-5115; costplus.com. Lamps Plus; 800/782-1967; lampsplus.com. Urban Outfitters; 800/282-2200; urbanoutfitters.com. *Paint:* Behr Process Corp. (Behr paint is available at Home Depot); 800/854-0133, ext. 2; website: behr.com. *Furniture and accessories:* Plummers Furniture; 310/837-0138. *Metal supplies:* Industrial Metal Supplies; 818/729-3333; imsmetals.com

PAGES 128–131, NATURAL CONNECTION; *Designers' Challenge,* episode 909
Photographer. Michael Garland
Designer. Ali Amani, NKBA, SIAP, Amani Design Inc., 562/421-1099; e-mail: amanidesign@earthlink.net; website: amanidesign.com
Resources. *Appliances:* Fisher & Paykel; 949/790-8900; website: fisherpaykel.com. *Faucets:* KWC Faucets; kwcfaucets.com. *Finishes:* Mimosa International Ltd.; 310/948-3385; website: mimosainternational.com. *Custom-designed glass:* Studio G3 Glass LLC; 604/517-8327; website: studiog3glass.com

PAGES 134–137, FLUENT FRENCH; *Designers' Challenge,* episode 903
Photographer. Michael Garland
Designer. Brian Klaas, ASID, BK Builders, 11101 Tuxford St., Sun Valley, CA 91352; 818/957-5777; website: brianklaas.com
Resources. *Flooring:* Lumber Liquidators; 800/356-6746; website: lumberliquidators.com. *Plumbing fixtures:* George's Pipe & Plumbing Supply Company; 626/792-5547; website: georgesshowroom.com. *Home appliances:* KitchenAid; 800/422-1230; website: kitchenaid.com. *Construction materials:* Weber Plywood & Lumber Co., Inc.; 714/259-1100 ext. 112; website: weberply.com. *Handpainted ceramics:* Lesal; 310/543-5430; website: lesal.com. *Knobs and pulls:* Anne at Home; email: custserve@anneathome.com. *Granite:* Marmi & Graniti Italiani (M.G.I. Inc.); 818/504-9594; email: Tony@mgiinc.mpowermail.com

PAGES 140–143, ECLECTIC BEAUTY; *Designers' Challenge,* episode 813
Photographer. Michael Garland
Designer. Bette Hornstein, Industry Partners, ASID., deZign services, 603 North Formosa Ave., Los Angeles, CA 90036; 323/935-9773; fax: 323/935-3519; e-mail: dzservices@sbcglobal.net

PAGES 146–149, MEDITERRANEAN EXPRESSIONS; *Designers' Challenge,* episode 806
Photographer. Michael Garland
Designer. Sandra Wisot, CID, Design Concepts Unlimited, 2134 Kenilworth Ave., Los Angeles, CA 90039; 323/664-3857; e-mail: sandrawisot@aol.com
Resources. *Tile:* Walker Zanger; 310/659-1234; website: walkerzanger.com. *Furnishings, accessories, and lighting:* Urban Archaeology; website: urbanarchaeology.com. *Natural stone:* Angelo & Sons Marble; 818/549-1877. *Kitchen and bath products:* Kitchen & Bath Expo; 626/599-9100. *Building materials:* Terry Sash & Door; 818/881-8738; website: terrylumber.com. *Antique reproduction lighting and hardware:* Rejuvenation Lighting & House Parts; 888/401-1900; website: rejuvenation.com. *Appliances and plumbing fixtures:* Pacific Sales; 310/357-2100; website: pacificsales.com. *Paint:* Dunn-Edwards Paints; 213/747-9441; 800/735-5762; website: dunnedwards.com

PAGES 152–155, COLORFUL COCINA; *Decorating Cents,* episode 2210
Photographer. Andy Lyons
Designers. *Decorating Cents* host Joan Steffand; Home and Garden Television; website: HGTV.com; and Barbara Sculati, Sculati Design, 1401 Valders Ave. North, Golden Valley, MN 55427; 763/544-9292; e-mail: sculatidesign@qwest.net; website: users.qwest.net/~sculati.
Resources. *Paint:* Glidden Company; 800/454-3336; website: gliddenpaints.com. Dutch Boy; website: dutchboy.com. *Spray paint:* Rust-Oleum Corp.; 800/553-8444; website: rustoleum.com. *Decorative project materials:* Menard's; 952/941-4400; website: menards.com. Michaels; 800/642-4235; website: michaels.com. Crafts Direct Outlet; 952/252-7043; Graham & Brown; website: grahambrown.com

INDEX

to some, inspiration comes naturally.
for the rest of us, may we suggest a good book?

©2004 Scripps Networks Inc.

Make that four good books. In all four, including the popular *Before & After Decorating*, *Design on a Dime*, and *Sensible Chic*, you'll find simple and affordable design ideas, not to mention plenty of inspiration from HGTV's expert designers. The newest addition, *Mission: Organization*, is full of tips on clearing the clutter from your home and getting organized.

YOU SHOULD SEE WHAT'S ON !

HGTV.com